THAXTED

in the

FOURTEENTH CENTURY

An Account

of the

Manor and Borough,

with

Translated Texts

by

K. C. NEWTON

Assistant Archivist

Published by

THE ESSEX COUNTY COUNCIL, CHELMSFORD

ESSEX RECORD OFFICE PUBLICATIONS, NO. 33

Printed by

J. H. CLARKE & CO., LTD., CHELMSFORD

1960

PREFACE

This book has its origins in a brief search of the documents translated at the end for any references to the cutlery industry in Thaxted. As will be seen in the *Introduction,* the search produced little or no positive evidence. It was obvious, however, that the survey of the manor made in 1393 was of exceptional value in presenting a picture of the manor both in its economic heyday and decline. By good fortune, positive evidence of a flourishing cutlery industry was found in another source.

It had been hoped to publish transcripts and translations of the survey and of the *compoti,* or bailiffs' accounts, but the further rise in printing costs precluded this if the book was to be offered at a reasonable price. In accordance with general editorial policy, that Essex Record Office Publications should be of use and interest to as large a number of people as possible, it was decided to omit the transcriptions. To meet the criticism that the work has less value to the scholar thereby, a microfilm has been made of the original records and of the typescript of line-for-line transcripts of the survey and of one of the *compoti.* Copies of the film may be had at low cost.

I am indebted to Mr. F. G. Emmison, F.S.A., F.R.Hist.S., the County Archivist, for continual encouragement and advice ; and to my colleagues, particularly to Miss Hilda Grieve, B.E.M., B.A., Senior Assistant Archivist, and Mr. A. C. Edwards, M.A., Lecturer in History in the Education Department, who have been invaluable critics and helpers. Warm thanks are also due to Mrs. Mildred Jacobs for her painstaking, accurate typing of the manuscript ; to Mr. J. C. W. Fulbeck for re-drawing my maps so excellently ; and to the printers, Messrs. J. H. Clarke & Co. for much helpful advice.

K. C. NEWTON

CONTENTS

Translations of

(*at end*)

THE MANOR OF THAXTED IN THE 14TH CENTURY

Introductory Note to the Sources

From the Conquest until the beginning of the 15th century the descent of the manor of Thaxted can be well established.[1] Its economic and social history before 1300, however, must remain in many respects obscure, for no manorial records of that period are known to have survived. Even for the 14th century there are no court rolls, only two surveys and three *compoti*, or bailiffs' accounts : but they are so detailed that the development of the manor in this period may be comprehensively traced and something of its previous history reasonably deduced. The earlier survey was made in 1348 upon the partition of the manor equally among the four coheirs of Giles de Badlesmere.[2] The other survey,[3] made in 1393, relates to three fourth parts of the manor, which by that time had become reunited under one lord.[4] The *compoti*, which relate to the years 1361-2, 1377-8 and 1380-1,[5] add much further detail.

The 1393 Survey consists of 12 membranes of parchment each 10½ inches wide, sewn head to tail, giving the roll an overall length of 28 feet ; there is writing on one side only. Despite its length, it is evident that the record is not complete, lacking a detailed summary of all demesne land held by lease ; only a beginning was made with the demesne gardens.[6] The *compoti* of 1361-2, 1377-8 and 1380-1 are each written on three membranes of parchment 10 inches in width giving them an overall length of 7 feet, 6½ feet and 7 feet respectively ; each has writing wholly on the face and on about one-third of the dorse. Translations of the Survey and of the *compoti* form the appendices to this study.

As no map of the manor is now known to exist, it has been necessary to plot detailed written surveys of the 16th and 17th centuries to establish its complicated bounds and to check this evidence with that of surviving records of other manors within the parish of Thaxted.[7]

All original sources and principal printed works consulted are listed at the end.

[1] See pp. 2-5.
[2] See *Calendar of Close Rolls,* 1346-1349, pp. 525-540, for full abstract.
[3] Essex Record Office, D/DHu M58.
[4] See p. 4.
[5] E.R.O., D/DHu M1.
[6] See p. 66.
[7] See sketch maps I-III at end.

I

THE DESCENT OF THE MANOR, 1066-1400

Before the Conquest Thaxted, one of the most valuable lordships in Essex,[8] had belonged to Wisgar, whose extensive possessions were granted by William to Richard FitzGilbert, one of his chief supporters and a kinsman.[9] From the most important of these estates, the lordship of Clare, the family which Richard founded was to derive its name[10]; and the seigniory of the many manors which he thus acquired became known as the Honour of Clare. Thaxted remained a possession of this great feudal family until sometime between 1307, when Gilbert de Clare, Earl of Gloucester and Hertford, had livery of his estates, though still a minor,[11] upon the death of his mother, Joan of Acre, daughter of Edward I,[12] and 1314, when on 24 June he met his death at Bannockburn. During this space of seven years he had alienated the manor to Bartholomew de Badlesmere.

Bartholomew, however, had apparently acquired it with other estates without licence of Edward II, an omission which he quickly remedied after the death of Earl Gilbert. On 2 July 1314, at Berwick upon Tweed, he sought of the King a pardon, which was granted on payment of a fine of £40.[13] Although Edward had shown him many favours, nevertheless he joined the Earl of Lancaster, with whom he had hitherto been on terms of enmity and hatred, in his rebellion. After the defeat at Boroughbridge on 16 March 1322, Bartholomew was captured, attainted and hanged as a traitor at Canterbury on 14 April following.[14] The estates of Badlesmere in common with those of the other rebels were taken into the King's hands and placed in the custody of Robert de Bures.[15] On 10 January 1324 he was ordered to deliver the manor of Thaxted to Arnold Calculi for a term of seven years. This was to compensate him for the termination of a lease for twelve years of the bailiwicks of Nautras in Aquitaine and 'Bagueneys'[16] with all their rents which he had been granted for services to Edward II and his father, and which had been worth £100 to him.[17] As was usual in such grants, rights of hunting and fishing were reserved to the Crown. It seems likely that Calculi lived at the manor house for a while, for in October 1324 he nominated William, vicar of Thaxted, as one of his two attorneys before going to Gascony in the royal service.[18]

[8] See p. 6.

[9] William I and Richard were both great-grandsons of Richard I of Normandy.

[10] For a concise account of the de Clare family, see article by J. Horace Round in *Dictionary of National Biography;* for individual members, see *The Complete Peerage sub* Clare, Gloucester and Hertford.

[11] He was born in 1291. His father, also Gilbert, Earl of Gloucester and Hertford, died in 1295.

[12] *Calendar of Patent Rolls,* 1307-1313, p. 10.

[13] *C.P.R.,* 1313-1317, p. 131.

[14] *The Complete Peerage, sub* Badlesmere.

[15] *Calendar of Close Rolls,* 1318-1323, p. 592.

[16] Either St. Pierre de Bassens, Gironde, or Bignay, Charente Inférieure.

[17] *C.P.R.,* 1321-1324, p. 361.

[18] *C.P.R.,* 1324-1327, p. 36.

With the accession of Edward III in 1327, and the temporary coming to power of his mother Isabella and Mortimer, redress was given at the Coronation Parliament to the rebels of 1322 who had survived and to the heirs and widows of those who had perished. Margaret, the widow of Bartholomew de Badlesmere, was accordingly granted her dower,[19] which included the manor of Thaxted. When, however, the sheriff of Essex sought to deliver possession of the manor to her, he was opposed, whereupon he was ordered to muster sufficient support in the county to enforce the delivery. The resistance had apparently been offered by the men of Hugh de Audley (who was in France taking part in the humiliating treaty negotiations with Charles IV) and his wife Margaret, who also laid claim to the manor. Before the sheriff could act upon the new command, the Audleys had turned to more peaceful and lawful means of asserting their alleged rights. Through their attorneys, they declared in Chancery that Bartholomew de Badlesmere had only been granted a life estate in the manor by Gilbert de Clare, and that it therefore belonged to Margaret as one of the sisters and coheirs of the Earl. Upon this complaint the order to the sheriff was countermanded, but Audley's attorneys then asserted that the sheriff still intended to deliver the manor to Lady Badlesmere under cover of a general writ, which made no specific mention of any properties. On 8 November 1327,[20] the sheriff was forbidden to execute any such writ in relation to the manor of Thaxted and ordered to send a transcript of the writ under seal to the King. A further order to him not to give possession of Thaxted to Lady Badlesmere made on 4 February 1328[21] indicates that Audley and his wife were still in possession.

The issue again came to trial in Chancery towards the end of the following June. After examining its own records the Court held that Bartholomew de Badlesmere and Margaret his wife had been granted an estate in the manor for life in survivorship and that Margaret de Audley was entitled to the reversion as part of her share in her late brother's lands. Accordingly the sheriff of Essex was again ordered to resume the manor into the King's hands, summoning such assistance in the county as he might need, and deliver it to Lady Badlesmere.[22] In the mandate to the sheriff made on 6 February 1329, to restore to Audley all his possessions in Essex,[23] the manor of Thaxted is specifically excepted.[24] It is doubtful, however, whether Lady Badlesmere actually obtained possession of the manor. Two years later, when Audley petitioned the King and his Council in Parliament for the restoration of those estates which he had not recovered in 1329, it was held that Thaxted had been in the possession of himself and his wife at the time of Lancaster's expedition; and it was decreed that they should have the manor again as they had it at the time of its seizure into the King's hands, saving the right of Margaret de Badlesmere 'when she will speak concerning it'. The sheriff was thereupon ordered to deliver it to them.[25]

[19] *Complete Peerage, sub* Badlesmere.
[20] *Calendar of Close Rolls,* 1327-1330, pp. 183, 184.
[21] *Ibid.,* p. 250.
[21] *C.C.R.,* 1327-1330, p. 297, 298.
[23] They had been seized upon his joining Lancaster's expedition against Mortimer which had ended in temporary compromise at Bedford in January.
[24] *C.C.R.,* 1327-1330, p. 435.
[25] *Ibid.,* 1330-1333, pp. 363, 364.

The final outcome of this fluctuating struggle between the Audleys and Badlesmere's widow does not now appear to be on record, but her son Giles was soon to establish not merely his mother's claim to a life inheritance but a claim to the fee simple of the manor in virtue of the pardon of 1314.[26] In 1330, before the last judgment in favour of Audley, Giles had obtained an exemplification of the pardon[27] and this, no doubt, represented the beginning of his part in the legal battle. In 1337 he further successfully laid claim to free warren in the demesne lands of Thaxted and other manors in virtue of the grant to his father in 1315.[28] Either by judicial decision or grant by Giles it was Audley who was to have only a life estate in the manor.[29]

Giles de Badlesmere died aged 24 between 7 April and 22 June 1338,[30] without issue, and his four sisters were found to be his coheirs.[31] They were Margery, wife of William de Ros, Lord Ros of Hamlake; Maud, wife of John de Vere, Earl of Oxford; Elizabeth, wife of William de Bohun, Earl of Northampton, and the former widow of Edmund de Mortimer; and Margaret, wife of John 2nd Lord Tibetot or Tiptoft. In the partition of the Badlesmere estates among the four coheirs the manor of Thaxted was physically divided on 21 December 1348.[32]

By this time the life estate of Hugh de Audley in the manor had terminated.[33] Margaret, wife of John Tiptoft, was also dead and her share of the manor vested in her son John, a minor, whose wardship had been granted to the Earl of Northampton.[34]

By 1360 the purparties of the manor granted to Margery, Maud and Elizabeth had become vested in Elizabeth's son, Roger de Mortimer, Earl of March,[35] then still a minor, for upon the death of William de Bohun, Earl of Northampton, in that year it was found that he had been holding of the King in chief three parts of the manor for life of the inheritance of his stepson, the King's ward, as parcel of the Earldom of Gloucester.[36] It was to be through the Earls of March that these three parts of the manor of Thaxted were to become vested in the Crown in the person of Edward IV.

The Tiptoft purparty of the manor, however, was to remain a separate entity for all time and was not to have a common owner with the remainder

[26] *Supra,* p. 2.

[27] *C.P.R.*, 1330-1334, p. 2.

[28] *C.P.R.*, 1334-1338, p. 554. The grant is enrolled on the Charter Roll for 1315 under date 12 August. Bartholomew de Badlesmere had also acquired at the same time the right to an annual fair at Thaxted, *Calendar of Charter Rolls,* 1300-1326, p. 283.

[29] *C.C.R.*, 1346-1349, p. 433.

[30] *Complete Peerage, sub* Badlesmere.

[31] *Calendar of Inquisitions post Mortem,* Vol. VIII, Edw. III, p. 127 *et seq.*

[32] *C.C.R.*, 1346-1349, pp. 525-540.

[33] He had died on 10 Nov. 1347, *Inq. p.m.*, Vol. IX, Edw. III, p. 56.

[34] *C.C.R.*, 1346-1349, p. 525.

[35] Through favour, though still a minor, Roger had succeeded in recovering the earldom, which had been forfeit on the execution of his grandfather Roger, the 1st Earl, in 1330.

[36] *Inq. p.m.*, Vol. X, Edw. III, p. 525. Roger de Mortimer also died in 1360 while taking part in Edward III's invasion of Burgundy. He was succeeded in the Earldom and in his estates by his only son Edmund.

of the manor until the 16th century.[37] On the death of Robert Tiptoft[38] on 13 April 1372, without male issue,[39] his estates were divided equally among his daughters Margaret aged 6, Millicent aged 4, and Elizabeth aged 2. The fourth part of the manor of Thaxted went to Elizabeth, later married to Philip le Despenser. He took livery of her inheritance on 23 November 1385.[40] This part of the manor thereafter came to be known as Spensers Fee.[41]

[37] Sir John Cutts, Under-Treasurer to Henry VIII.
[38] Robert was the younger brother and heir of John Tiptoft, who died a minor.
[39] *Inq. p.m.*, Vol. XIII, Edw. III, pp. 190-195.
[40] *The Complete Peerage, sub* Despenser.
[41] For the subsequent descent of the manor of Thaxted with Spensers Fee, see Philip Morant's *History and Antiquities of Essex* (1768), Vol. II, pp. 436-439.

II

THE EVOLUTION OF THE MANOR FROM THE 11TH TO THE 14TH CENTURY

At the time of the Domesday Survey Thaxted was one of the most valuable lordships in the county, having a geldable value of £50, an increase of £20 over its value in the reign of the Confessor and at the Conquest. This figure of £50 is equal to that given for Walden, the largest and most populous of the north-west Essex manors.[1] But while the rise in value of Walden from £36 in 1066 to £50 in 1086 has been reasonably explained,[2] this is not so easy in the case of Thaxted. At Walden a significant increase in population and in the number of ploughteams coupled with a reduction in woodland for swine of one-fifth[3] is sufficient evidence of agricultural expansion. The amount of woodland for swine in these manors was equal at both dates,[4] suggesting that clearance was going on at the same rate; but at Thaxted, population declined very slightly and the number of ploughs decreased sharply.[5] Moreover, the Survey states specifically (and most unusually) that the stock could be increased by 16 ploughs, which would restore the number to the level in 1066. The increase in sheep and beehives and the addition of a second mill could only account for a part of the increased value. The accuracy of the figure of £50 is confirmed in the Survey, for it adds that 'Richard has given it on lease (*ad censum*) to a certain Englishman at 60 pounds; but he loses (*deficiunt illi*) at least 10 pounds every year'. Thaxted is by no means an isolated example of such an increase in value accompanied by a decrease of both woodland and number of ploughteams,[7] but the evidence of Domesday is too meagre to solve this difficult, intriguing problem.

DOMESDAY STATISTICS OF THAXTED

Areas	*1066*	*1086*
Manor	9½ hides[6] (1,140 acres)	9½ hides (1,140 acres)
Land held by 3 sokemen	2 hides 15 acres (255 acres)	2 hides 15 acres (255 acres)
Land held by 1 sokeman	7½ acres	7½ acres (taken into manor)
	11½ hides, 22½ acres (1,402½ acres)	11½ hides, 22½ acres (1,402½ acres)

[1] Walden contained 19½ hides, Thaxted 9½ hides.

[2] *Saffron Walden and its Environs*, by Mrs. D. Monteith (unpublished M.A. thesis, University of London, 1958), pp. 63-70. Copy in E.R.O.

[3] From sufficient for 1,000 to sufficient for 800 swine.

[4] See Table below.

[5] *Ibid.*

[6] There is good evidence that in the Essex Domesday 1 hide = 120 acres. See *V.C.H., Essex*, Vol. I. (1907).

[7] See *V.C.H., Essex*, Vol. I (1907), pp. 364-365.

		1066	1086
Plough Teams			
Demesne		8	7
Men		34	18
Sokemen		4	3½
		46	28½
Tenants			
Villeins	of the Lord	55	52
Bordars		24	24
Serfs		16	16
Villeins	of three Sokemen	10	2
Bordars		2	10
Serfs		4	—
		111	104
Woodland			
Manor		for 1,000 swine	for 800 swine
3 Sokemen		—	50
		for 1,000 swine	for 850 swine
Meadow			
Manor			120 acres
3 Sokemen			34 acres
			154 acres
Mill			
Manor		1	2
Animals			
Rounceys	of the Lord	4	4
Beasts		36	36
Swine		128	128
Sheep		200	320
Beehives		10	16
Value			
Manor		£30	£50
3 Sokemen			£ 6

At the time of the Survey the only other manor in Thaxted was Yerdelai (now Yardley), a small estate in the north of the parish held by Tihel the Breton *alias* Tihel de Helion.[8] By the 14th century, an unrecorded process of subinfeudation had carved a number of submanors out of the manor of Thaxted. The largest was Horham Hall,[9] with its lands principally in the western part of the parish and in neighbouring Broxted, but with other lands scattered about the parish including a fairly large tract on the eastern border.[10] It is likely that the estate held by the heirs of Walter de Acre in Thaxted and Broxted in 1262 was this manor,[11] and William de Wauton, who held it by

[8] *Ibid.*, p. 541.

[9] The Lord of Horham Hall rendered Wardpence to Thaxted, see p. 57.

[10] See sketch map II.

[11] Morant, *History and Antiquities of Essex* (1768), Vol. II, p. 440.

the name of Horham at the time of his death in 1347,[12] had been granted free warren in all his demesne lands of Thaxted and 'Chaure' (now Broxted) in 1289.

Priors Hall, the manor of the rectory of Thaxted, formed part of the possessions of the College of Stoke until the Dissolution. Before the Conquest the rectory had belonged to the collegiate church of St. John the Baptist of Clare, which in 1124 was removed by Richard de Clare to Stoke nearby and raised to the status of a college.[13] Little is known about Priors Hall before the 15th century, before which date no manorial records are known to exist, though there are oblique references to it in the Survey of 1393.[14] Its lands were situate to the south of the town on either side of the road to Dunmow,[15] and it had property near the vicarage in what was to become known as Newbiggin Street.[16]

The manor of Richmonds apparently arose out of the lands and privileges granted by the Earls of Clare to successive keepers of the three parks in Thaxted.[17] An undated charter of Richard de Clare, Earl of Gloucester and Hertford, which is enrolled upon the 1393 Survey,[18] possibly records the beginnings of this manor. Certainly it was the earliest document known to the compilers of the Survey. Part of its lands were in Thaxted Great Park and the rest were scattered in the southern part of the parish; a number of dwellings in what came to be known as Newbiggin Street were also held of this manor.[19]

Of the small manors or reputed manors of FitzRalph, Venors and Stanfold Garden mentioned by Morant,[20] little or nothing is known. Venors, however, which was part of the possessions of Tilty Abbey, is to be identified with the messuage and 60 acres of land and meadow ascribed to the Abbot in the 1393 Survey.[21] Coldhams Fee, of which a number of properties in Bolford Street were held, is not found in records before the 16th century.[22]

By the middle of the 14th century a comparatively large urban settlement had grown up near the manor house and church, mainly extending southwards down the hill towards and over the stream which crossed the main thoroughfare.[23] A part of the township had acquired the status of a *burgus*, which separated it administratively, though not legally, from the manor, and which conferred upon certain of its inhabitants a special free condition—a sure indication that the economy of Thaxted had an important commercial and industrial basis, apart from agriculture.[24]

On the west side of the main street, just below the church, stood the great outer gateway 'with chambers above and below', which led into the

[12] *Inq. p.m.*, Vol. VIII, Edw. III, p. 506.
[13] Morant, *op. cit.*, Vol. II, p. 443.
[14] See pp. 35, 36.
[15] See sketch map II.
[16] See sketch map III and p. 44 below.
[17] The very incomplete account of the descent of this manor given by Morant, *op. cit.*, Vol. II, p. 440, and followed by subsequent historians of Essex, appears to be quite inaccurate.
[18] See p. 43.
[19] See sketch map III.
[20] *Op. cit.*, pp. 440-441.
[21] See p. 45.
[22] See sketch map III.
[23] See sketch map III.
[24] See pp. 20-21.

outer courtyard of the manor house. Around this courtyard were the principal outbuildings—the 'great stable', the grange, the smithy and another stable adjoining, the granary, bakery and brewery, 'la Pressourhous' where wine was pressed, the 'pundfold' and pigsty. Entry to the 'great hall' and the other buildings of the main range was through an inner gateway, near which was a building called 'Knightes Chamber', and across the inner court. Possibly forming a single unit with the great hall and its contiguous domestic offices, there was a great upper chamber with rooms beneath it and the 'Countesses Chambre'. A separate building in the inner court was 'Quarelles-hall' with a number of smaller chambers at either end of it, and likely to have been the building where the courts of the manor were held. Across a court on the south side of the great hall there was another exit from the manor house through the gate at the head of 'Swynfordeschambre' and into Park Street.[25]

About the main buildings and between them and the river Chelmer were the gardens, 'Countesse Gardyn', 'Bolforde Gardyn' and 'la Burton'. In all, the site of the manor contained almost 18 acres.[26]

Around the town were the great open fields, five in number, but worked as three.[27] Of these, 'Northfelde', 'Worthen', 'Boxstede' and 'Asshefelde' possibly have their origins in the pre-Conquest period, though their extent was no doubt greatly increased after the coming of the Normans.[28] 'Newe-felde' may represent the clearance of woodland begun at a post-Conquest date. It is not possible to give the precise acreages of these open fields, for the Surveys of 1348 and 1393 do not, except in minor cases, assign the proportions of tenants' holdings to them. Moreover, from abuttals, it is clear that at least some of the sub-manors worked the fields in common with the parent manor. This is further supported by the evidence of the very detailed 16th and 17th century surveys,[29] where the vestigial remains of open field cultivation are shown to belong to more than one manor.[30] The demesne holdings in these fields in the 14th century suggest their extent. 'Northfelde' with 'Worthen', 352 acres; 'Asshefelde', 442 acres; and 'Boxstede' with 'Newefelde', 366 acres.[31]

Along the banks of the Chelmer, which flows generally north to south through the centre of the parish, and along one of its tributaries flowing south-west to join it on the south-west outskirts of the town, were the common meadows and pastures. Additional pasturage for the cattle lay in the large green at the hamlet of Bardfield End to the east of the town and to a lesser extent in Cutlers Green to the west and Richmonds Green to the south-east.

[25] This description is based principally on the evidence of the Survey (Partition), 1348. *C.C.R.*, 1346-1349, pp. 525-540.

[26] See p. 33.

[27] See sketch map I and pp. 34-36.

[28] The extent of Thaxted including Yardleys (1 hide) at Domesday was only just over 12½ hides (1,522½ acres) or about a quarter of the later parish. In the 14th century the demesne holdings of the manor of Thaxted alone in the open fields was 1,160 acres. See pp.

[29] See List of Sources, p. 103.

[30] These remnants of the former open fields were still to be seen on the 1st edition 6-inch O.S. map, 1881.

[31] See pp. 34-36.

The extensive parks and woods of the manor were a constant reminder that the land was once almost entirely forest.[32] Great Park or South Frith, with an area of over 650 acres,[33] covered much of the south-east part of the parish. From the gardens behind the manor house as far as Cutlers Green stretched the Little Park, some 160 acres in extent.[34] Lastly, in the extreme east of the parish, there were the 179 acres of 'Oldefrith', perhaps the first area of woodland to be deliberately retained as such.

Although since Domesday a considerable body of freeholders had risen upon the manor of Thaxted, an analysis of their holdings shows that their equality of status before the law had no economic equivalent.[35]

Freeholdings in 1348[36]

Size of Holding	*Number of such Holdings*
82 acres	1
71	1
60	3
32	1
30	1
21	1
18	1
15	1
12	5
9	2
8	1
6	4
5	1
4	3
3	5
2¾	1
2	9
1½	5
1¼	1
1	15
¾	3
½	2
¼	1

[32] See p. 39.

[33] See p. 39. This accords closely with the joint acreage of Richmonds and Lodge Farms, formed out of the park in the 16th century, given in the Tithe Award, 1846 (E.R.O., D/CT 348). For deeds relating to the alienation and disparking of the Great Park in the 16th century, see E.R.O., D/DGh T27.

[34] This too was disparked and alienated in the 16th century (E.R.O., D/DGh T27) and comprises the greater part of modern Park Farm.

[35] A number of freeholders were labourers, see p. 17.

[36] In addition to the holdings given below, the survey lists a number of holdings without specifying the acreages, viz., messuages, 5; tenements, 3; curtilages, 2; cottages, 1; crofts, 1; parcels, plots or pieces of land, 10; purprestures, 19. Most of these are obviously very small holdings, and from the rents of those where this is not immediately apparent, e.g. 'messuages' and 'tenements', they were all small.

Despite the disparity in the size of the freeholds, the figures suggest that there was at an earlier period a greater uniformity in their size, at least among those of larger extent. One of the 60-acre farms and those of 30 acres and 15 acres are described as two virgates, one virgate and half a virgate respectively in the 1348 Survey, the virgate being a unit of measurement usually associated with the more uniform villein holdings. It is also possible that some of the smaller holdings represent virgates which had been subdivided a number of times, as a result of the greater liberty to alienate possessed by the freeholder. Some of the freeholds may represent villein land which had been enfranchised. In this respect, it is noteworthy that the half virgate, also so described in the 1393 Survey,[37] was charged with the service of three carriages[38] of corn and hay for the lord, though cartage service is not an uncommon obligation attaching to manorial freeholders. No other freeholder on the manor of Thaxted was charged with this particular service, but the tenant of a messuage and 20 acres of land and 1 acre of meadow held his land free of rent provided that he acted as the lord's swineherd, in default of which he paid an annual rent of 4s.[39]

In a special class were those freeholders who in return for their lands had duties connected with the three parks of the manor. The office of keeping the parks, held by the service of serjeanty, was no ordinary service to render, as the terms of the charter granted by Richard de Clare in the middle of the 13th century make clear.[40] Not only did the office secure to its holder the largest free estate within the manor, but eventually, at some time after the granting of the charter, the holding acquired the status of a manor, which was to take its name from the Richmond family, whose members were the parkers of Thaxted in the 14th and 15th centuries.[41] The keeper of the gates of South Frith or Great Park and the two keepers of the gates of Little Park paid no money rent for their dwellings and small holdings. Instead they maintained the enclosures of the parks, as well as attending the gates. The gatekeeper of South Frith had to keep in good state the hedge about the park and received 1d. for every perch renewed and any dead wood removed. Those of the Little Park had to repair any faults in its fence, receiving 1d. for every perch of fencing renewed, but nothing if this entailed merely replacing one or two palings. They were also charged with bringing to safety any who lost their way in the park at night.[42]

Just as there was great disparity in the size of freeholdings, so there was apparently no relationship among the rents they paid. Of the three holdings each of 60 acres, one paid an annual rent of 20s., another 4s., and the third

[37] See p. 47.

[38] Described as 'half carriages' in the 1348 Survey (Partition), *C.C.R.*, 1346-1349, p. 528.

[39] See p. 46.

[40] See pp. 8, 43-44.

[41] That the messuage and 80 acres assigned to the office of parker of Thaxted and the other lands held by John Richmond, junior, in the 1393 Survey are to be identified with the manor of Richmonds is further confirmed by 16th century deeds of the manor in the E.R.O. (D/DGh T27) and surviving manorial records (court rolls 1605-1641, 1623; rental, 1682; D/DHw M2; D/DBa M8; D/DK M149).

[42] See p. 44.

8s. 10d.[43] A messuage and 30 acres of land yielded 7s.[44] A glance at either Survey will rapidly establish that in holdings of few acres there was the same wide variation of rents. A number of freeholders were also charged with the payment of rents in kind. From seven came a total of 13 capons, and from two, 3 ploughshares; while others paid two hens, 4 geese, 1 pound of cumin and 7 arrows respectively.[45] Of these the parker of Thaxted had to provide 2 chickens, 2 capons and 4 geese, by far the heaviest burden.[46]

A peculiarity among the freeholds of the manor of Thaxted was the five small holdings situated some ten miles away in the parish of Haverhill on the Essex-Suffolk border.[47] The manor of Haverhill, like Thaxted, was a possession of the Clare family, but there is no evidence to explain these 'detached parts' of the latter. Quit rents from the Haverhill freeholds were still being paid to the lord of Thaxted at the end of the 16th century,[48] but not apparently at a later date.

The tenants of lands in villeinage also formed legally a single class, characterised by the unfree nature of their tenure, their dependance upon the lord of the manor and their unavoidable obligations towards him. Economically they fell into five classes, of which four—virgaters and half-virgaters, akermen, coterells and cotmen—may be distinguished from each other solely by the relative size of their holdings; the fifth—the molmen—is to be distinguished from the others not by the amount of land which its members individually held but by the privileged nature of the services by which they held their lands.

It is the molmen who were socially the elite of the *nativi tenentes*. Unlike the holdings of their fellow villeins, theirs had no overall uniformity.

Molmen Holdings[49]

Size of Holding	*No. of such Holdings*
77 acres	1
1 virgate	1
¾ virgate (*3 quartrone*)	1
½ virgate	7
14 acres	1
¼ virgate (*quartrona*)	5

[43] Survey (Partition), 1348. *C.C.R.* 1346-1349, pp. 535, 539. As to two of them, Survey, 1393, pp. 45, 46. The 20s. virgate of 1348 rendered a rent of only 5s. 8d. in 1393.

[44] *Ibid.*, pp. 532, 539.

[45] Of these the payment of 7 arrows and 1 ploughshare belonged to the fourth part of the manor not represented in the 1393 Survey below. For these see 1348 Survey (Partition), *C.C.R.*, 1346-1349, p. 539.

[46] See p. 44.

[47] Survey (Partition), 1348. *C.C.R.*, 1346-1349, pp. 528, 536, 539. As to three of the holdings, see pp. 47-48.

[48] See, for instance, Survey, 1593. D/DHu M23A.

[49] The molmen holdings in the three quarters of the manor represented by the 1393 Survey (pp. 48-53) are fortunately grouped together under one heading, but to identify those of the other fourth part (Tiptoft purparty, later Spensers Fee) it was necessary to collate closely the 1393 Survey with the 1348 Survey (Partition). By this means it was established that molmen holdings appear at the end of each assignment. Since the absolute number of villein holdings in each class (other than that of molmen) is known from the surviving *compoti* (pp. 67-102) which relate to the *whole* manor, it was determinable that the last four villein holdings of the Tiptoft purparty were of molmen and they are included in the above table.

Size of Holding	*No. of such Holdings*
8 acres	1
Croft and 7 acres	1
7 acres	5
6 acres	2
5 acres	1
4 acres	1
3 acres	1
2 acres	2
½ acre	1

It is possible that some of the smaller holdings represent former units which had become subdivided. But if this is so, it suggests that the molmen had greater freedom to alienate, for such fragmentation is not to be found in the holdings of the other classes of villeins. None of the surviving records, however, helps in deciding this point.

The 1393[50] Survey shows that the molmen did not always render equal services for similar-sized holdings, nor did those with smaller holdings necessarily perform services directly proportionate to those of a larger one. Thus, in return for his 77 acres, the tenant of this largest molmen estate had only to plough a total of 9 acres of demesne or pay 6s. to the lord instead.[51] The holder of the virgate had also to plough 9 acres of demesne for which he received 3d. an acre from the lord ; but he had further to provide on three days yearly a cart, two horses and two men to carry oats or pease, for which service he received 3d. a day ; to work at harvest for eight days called 'bederipdayes',[52] during which time he received daily from the lord a loaf (whereof 10 to the bushel), ¾d. of cheese, and potage ; and to make ready for the cart one 'bedeacre',[53] for which he got two loaves.

The four tenants of half virgates[54] were each required to provide for half a day a cart, two horses and two men to cart hay and for another half-day to cart oats or pease receiving from the lord a ½d. ; to work on 4 'bederipdayes', getting daily the same allowance of food as the virgater ; and to make ready for the cart 1 'bedehalfacre', receiving a loaf. Two of the half virgaters had also to help to make the lord's hay. These services do not represent a half part of those performed by the virgater either in their nature or in their value.[55]

Although he held less land than the virgater, the tenant who held the three quarterlands had not only to give the same services but had also to help with the lord's hay, providing two men, one equipped with an iron fork.[56]

Apart from two seven-acre molmen who had to perform the same services as the half virgaters,[57] the other four each having seven-acre holdings,

[50] Unfortunately the 1348 Survey (Partition) does not give services in detail : therefore the exact details of the services of the villeins of the Tiptoft purparty (later Spensers Fee) remain unknown.

[51] See p. 52.

[52] 'bederipdayes', i.e., days spent in reaping.

[53] 'bedeacre', i.e. gathering, binding and stooking an acre of corn or pease.

[54] See pp. 49, 50, 51.

[55] The net value of the virgater's services was 8s. 9d. ; those of the half virgaters had a net value of 2s. 6d., or 3s. 2d. if haymaking was also done.

[56] See p. 49.

[57] See pp. 49, 50.

the five with quarterlands, the two tenants of two-acre holdings, the respective holders of four acres, of 'Mellerslonde' (1 acre),[58] and of a half acre, all did the same services.[59] Each had to assist with the haymaking, work four 'bederippes', and prepare for the cart a 'bedehalfacre', a burden scarcely less onerous than that borne by the half virgaters. One molman holding a quarterland had also to help make the haycocks[60] and another having two acres had to attend to the hedges of the (great) park.[61]

Of the remaining molmen, the holder of five acres (apparently composed of two former holdings of three acres and two acres respectively) had only to help make the lord's hay in one of the common meadows with one man and prepare for the cart one 'bederode'[62] for which he received half a loaf as sustenance. The three holdings of six acres had no services charged upon them at all.[63] But there is no reason to suppose that they were freeholds which molmen chanced to hold, for in two cases the lands are said to be held *in bondagio*.[64] Nor can they be regarded as examples of early commutation of services, for the rents were in each instance unusually low.

It is also noticeable that the money rents rendered by the molmen had no uniformity. Just as he was privileged in the matter of services so was the tenant of the largest holding (the toft and 77 acres) by this tenure paying a comparatively low rent. His rent of 7s. 6d.[65] was just 6d. greater than that paid by the tenant of the virgate.[66] The five holders of a quarterland rendered rents which varied between 1s. 6d. and 4s. 8d.[67]; the four half virgaters rents of 6s. 2d., 3s. 10d., 4s. 6d. and 4s.[68]

The clue to the principal distinction between the molmen and the other bondmen, however, does not lie in the Surveys of 1348 and 1393, at least not obviously, but in the surviving *compoti*. In them it will be found that the bailiff never accounted for the labour services due, either theoretically or actually, from the molmen, as he did for the other bondmen.[69] Like others with the same privileged status on many other manors, the molmen of Thaxted formed a pool of labour which was only called upon by the lord in an emergency to plough the demesne in winter or to gather the harvest. And if they were not so called on they did not have to pay a cash equivalent for the services unperformed as did the other bondmen.[70]

The bondmen described in the 1393 Survey as 'virgaters and half-virgaters'[71] held between them a total of 7¾ virgates or 232½ acres.[72] In all there were 14 holdings, two each of 1 virgate, eleven each of ½ virgate, and a single quarterland.[73]

[58] According to 1348 Survey (Partition), *C.C.R.*, 1346-1349, p. 530.
[59] See pp. 50, 51, 52.
[60] See p. 51.
[61] See p. 50.
[62] i.e. a quarter of a 'bedeacre'.
[63] See pp. 51, 52.
[64] See p. 51.
[65] See p. 52.
[66] See p. 48.
[67] The rents were 1s. 6d., 2s., 4s. 5d., 4s. 8d., and 2s. See pp. 50, 51, 52.
[68] See pp. 49, 50, 51.
[69] See pp. 73-75, 86-88, 100-102.
[70] *Cf.* Vinogradoff, *Villainage in England* (1892), pp. 183-186.
[71] See pp. 53-54.
[72] See pp. 74, 87, 100.
[73] The holdings by this tenure in the quarter part of the manor not represented in the 1393 Survey below were three ½ virgates which are the first bond holdings listed in Tiptoft purparty in the 1348 Survey (Partition), *C.C.R.*, 1346-1349, p. 540, and a quarter part of one of the whole virgates, see p. 54.

With these bondmen is found the equality of burden of labour service which is usually associated with base tenure. The virgater had to plough 24 acres of demesne or give to the lord 4d. per acre. Between Michaelmas (29 September) and the Feast of the Nativity of St. John the Baptist (24 June) he could expect to do one 'work' daily from Monday to Friday unless a feast day occurred,[74] or pay ½d. for each 'work' not performed[75]; from the Nativity of St. John to Lammas Day (1 August) and from thence to Michaelmas 10 'works' might have to be carried out every week or 1d. paid for each one not demanded by the lord. He had also to mow 9 acres of the lord's meadow if need be, but if this service were done he was allowed to offset for each acre mown two of the works due from him; and a further remission of 8 works was made if he were called upon to give additional help with the hay harvest, without regard for the number of days worked. At harvest time he carried out 8 'bederippes' and made ready one 'bedeacre' for the cart, receiving the same food allowance as the molmen.[76] On three days he had to provide a cart, two horses and two men to carry oats or pease, for which he received 3d. a day from the lord. Each year the virgater had also to give to the lord, on demand, 3 quarters of malt or 3d. in lieu of each quarter. The services of the half-virgaters and the holder of the quarterland were in direct proportion to those of the virgater.

With the 'akermen' there is found a complete uniformity in size of holdings and services.[77] Each of the nine holdings was of 10 acres of land, and its tenant was charged with two weekly works between Michaelmas and the Feast of the Nativity of St. John the Baptist or had to pay ½d. for each work not done, but unlike the virgaters and half-virgaters the akerman received no allowance for feast days in this period other than the fifteen days of Christmas and the weeks of Easter and Pentecost. In the period from the Feast of the Nativity of St. John until Lammas Day, when two works weekly could be demanded or 1d. a work paid instead,[78] no allowance was made for festivals. From the akermen no works were demanded between Lammas Day and Michaelmas, though the burden of each at harvest was as heavy as that of the half virgater (4 'bederippes' and the preparation of 1 'bedehalfacre' for the cart), and no allowance of works was made for helping with a man to mow all the lord's hay or for the days which they might spend making the haycocks.

The holdings of the eleven 'coterells' show a certain variety of size though the majority had an area of an acre.

[74] See p. 53.

[75] See p. 18 for the significance of the term 'work'.

[76] See p. 13.

[77] See p. 55. It is obvious that the two 'akermen' assigned to the Tiptoft purparty in the 1348 Survey (Partition) performed the same services as the seven recorded in the 1396 Survey, for the gross value of their rents and services is the same (*C.C.R.*, 1346-1349, p. 540). Note that in 1348 two 'akermen' holdings were held by one tenant in the Tiptoft purparty, as were two assigned to the Bohun purparty (*Ibid.*, p. 537; below, p. 55).

[78] For significance of the 'work', see p. 18.

'Coterell' Holdings[79]

Size of Holding	*No. of such Holdings*
Messuage and 7 acres	1
Toft and 2 acres 1 rood	1
Messuage and 1 acre 1 rood of land and piece of pasture	1
Messuage and 1 acre[80] and other unspecified land	1
Messuage and 1 acre[81]	7

It is likely, however, that the original 'Coterellonds' were quite uniform, for the messuage and 7 acres and the messuage and 2 acres 1 rood of the 1393 Survey[82] are respectively described in the 1348 Partition as a 'messuage and an acre of land and 6 acres of land formerly of John Fromond' and 'a messuage, 1 acre of land and another acre of land and a rood'.[83] This suggests that the lands of the coterells in excess of one acre represent additional grants by the lord for which more rent but no extra services were demanded. The completely uniform labour services and the varying rents owed by the coterells strengthens this supposition.[84]

The coterells had each to perform weekly between Michaelmas and the Feast of the Nativity of St. John the Baptist one work valued at ½d., and thence to Michaelmas one work weekly valued at 1d., with no allowance for festivals other than the fifteen days at Christmas and the weeks of Easter and Pentecost. They had also to help with the mowing of the lord's hay and at harvest to do 4 'bederippes' and to make ready a 'bedehalfacre' for the cart.

The cotmen[85] were little different from the coterells, save that their services were somewhat less onerous. Their holdings were six in number,[86] of which five were 1 acre in extent and the sixth 3 acres. This last no doubt represents an original holding of one acre to which two acres had been added for an increased money rent but no extra services. Again, there was a uniformity of labour services; every cotman had to do one work weekly, valued at 1d., only at the busiest time of the year between Lammas Day and Michaelmas, and also to work four 'bederippes' and to make ready a 'bedehalfacre' for the cart. At haymaking they had to help to mow all the lord's meadows until the task was complete and to make the haycocks.

[79] Based on the 1393 Survey and 1348 Survey (Partition) (for Tiptoft purparty), *C.C.R.*, 1346-1349, p. 540.

[80] A holding assigned to Tiptoft in 1348 Partition.

[81] Includes 4 holdings assigned to Tiptoft in 1348 Survey (Partition) and two described as 'Coterellond' in 1393 Survey (p. 56), but which the Partition denotes as being each of 1 acre in extent.

[82] See pp. 55, 56.

[83] *C.C.R.*, 1346-1349, p. 529. John Fromond had been hanged for felony in about 1304 and his land had escheated to the lord. See *C.C.R.*, 1302-1307, p. 286, for livery of certain of his lands to William de Wauton (who was lord of Horham Hall).

[84] See pp. 55-56.

[85] See pp. 56-57.

[86] Two of these, each consisting of a messuage and 1 acre of land, were assigned to the Tiptoft purparty in the 1348 Survey (Partition), *C.C.R.*, 1346-1349, p. 540.

It was also a general custom of the manor that every bondman who owned a plough either solely or jointly with his neighbour should come for a day to each of the great open fields to plough the demesne, the lord in return providing a meal. Similarly he was to come to haulm with the lord for a day for a like reward. On the half day which he spent gathering nuts for the lord there could be no pleasurable anticipation of a meal at the end, nor indeed any reward at all.[87]

The labour services appear to be heavy, particularly in the case of the virgater and half-virgater, though one can discern here, perhaps, an implementation of the maxim 'from each according to his ability'. It was the larger bondman, if anyone, who could afford to employ others to do his services, if no adult members of his own family were available. The lowly coterells and cotmen and the tenants of small freehold and burgage plots, whose holdings could at no time have afforded even a subsistence standard of living, must have always formed a pool of labour from which the more wealthy tenants could draw. Of forty-one labourers listed in the Poll Tax Return of 1381,[88] five may be identified with occupiers of small bond holdings and eight with tenants of small free and burgage holdings in the 1393 Survey.

Apart from his ability to employ labour, an analysis of the *compoti*[89] reveals that the burden of works upon the virgater and half-virgater was not quite as heavy as the 1393 Survey would suggest. Not only did they receive a remission of summer works for haymaking,[90] as the Survey records, but also an allowance of winter works if ploughing was performed, at the rate of 2½ works per acre ploughed.[91] The theoretical total of winter works which the virgater could be called upon to do was 190.[92] By doing his ploughing service he was allowed 60 off this total; the festivals of Christmas, Easter and Pentecost gave a regular bonus of 20 works not to be performed; and a number of other feast days, variable according to the year, meant a further reduction.[93] Thus the *compotus* for 1361-2 allows to the virgater 23 winter works in respect of feast days; in 1377-8 and 1380-1 the totals were 14 and 18.[94] In summer and autumn, it is true, he could not look for so much relief, as the Church was apparently not unmindful of the needs of agriculture in relation to the fixing of saints days and festivals. In 1362 only 5 feast days fell on working days in the summer and 7 in the autumn; in 1378 the numbers were 3 and 5, and in 1382, 2 in each period.[95] This remission of works on festival days does not imply any strict observance by the lords of Thaxted of the Canon Law which forbade work on holy days: as already noted,[96] this mitigation of week work only applied to the virgaters and half-virgaters. Indeed, there is little evidence that many lords of manors observed the

[87] See p. 57.

[88] P.R.O., E179/107/49. Where identification is possible, the description of each tenant in the 1393 Survey given in the Poll Tax Return has been incorporated in the Index of Persons.

[89] See pp. 67-102.

[90] See p. 53.

[91] See pp. 74, 87, 100.

[92] See pp. 74, 87, 100.

[93] See p. 53.

[94] See pp. 74, 87, 100-101.

[95] See pp. 74-75, 87-88, 101-102.

[96] See pp. 15, 16.

canonical injunction, least of all on manors owned by ecclesiastical corporations.[97]

A consideration of the term 'work' will also support the view that the burden of manual labour for the lord did not press quite so hardly upon any of the bondmen as a superficial study of the surveys and *compoti* might suggest. It is clear that when the virgater of Thaxted was said to have to work each week in the winter from Monday to Friday,[98] this did not mean that he spent the whole of each day labouring on the demesne. Simple arithmetic will show that this could not have been so, for in summer and autumn 10 works a week were due from him to the lord.[99] At the most a winter work entailed labouring half a day and probably for fewer hours, for the ploughing of only an acre of land brought an allowance of 2½ works; also the summer and autumn work, which clearly does not imply a whole day's labour, since two were demanded of the virgater daily, was valued at 1d. compared with ½d. for the winter work. This valuation, however, may reflect the value of half a day's work in summer or autumn compared with half a day's work in winter, so that a winter work is not necessarily to be equated with a quarter of a working day.

In harvest time, the five-day week of the virgater, it is true, could be extended if the lord required the boon works termed in Thaxted 'bederippes' and 'bedeacres'.[100] Unlike some manors, however, the maximum number of boon works which could be customarily demanded from any bondman was certain.[101]

Without suggesting that the Thaxted bond tenants' labour services were not burdensome, a closer examination of the evidence reveals a picture of manorial labour less grim than has sometimes been painted.[102] Nor was the lord entirely unaware of the expediency of giving some recompense to his tenants at the busiest time of the year. In addition to providing food when boon services were worked,[103] drink was made available whenever autumn works were done.[104] And at Thaxted there was the widespread custom of the lord rewarding the haymakers with a sheep[105] when the task was finished. Known at Thaxted as 'madram',[106] it would appear to have been a local form of the custom, whereby a ram was released into the meadow and the haymakers had then to chase and capture the animal before they could bear it away as a reward for their hard work.

Some of the tenants' time was taken in other ways. The virgaters and half-virgaters, the akermen, coterells and cotmen were all liable to be elected reeve or hayward.[107] The molmen,[108] as in other respects, were different: some had to be ready to serve in both offices, others, the one or the other. A very few appear to have been exempt from this service, notably the holder

[97] See H. S. Bennett, *Life on the English Manor,* 1150-1400 (Cambridge, 1938), pp. 115-118.

[98] See p. 53.

[99] *Ibid.*

[100] See p. 13.

[101] See pp. 15-16.

[102] See also H. S. Bennett, *op. cit.*, p. 104, on this point.

[103] See pp. 13, 15.

[104] See p. 53.

[105] H. S. Bennett, *op. cit.*, p. 111.

[106] See pp. 71, 84, 97.

[107] See pp. 53-57.

[108] See pp. 48-53.

of the toft and 77 acres, the largest holding. Analysis, however, shows that the size of holdings is not the key to the differentiation among the molmen. No doubt those who were exempt from either or both of these offices counted it as a privilege, for they, particularly that of reeve, were responsible and onerous. The reeve was the *Johannes Factotum* of the manor and might be answerable for every conceivable aspect of the manorial organisation, from arranging the work in the fields and superintending his fellow bondmen doing their labour services, to managing the sale of produce in local and even distant markets and inspecting the state of repair of buildings.[109] The office of reeve might give him the status of head bondman for a year, or longer if re-elected, but it must have needed a strong personality, self-confidence and some organising ability, for the risks of annoying his fellows on the one hand or of angering the lord, his steward or bailiff on the other were manifold. For this reason it is remarkable that, apart from some molmen, every bondman was liable for this duty. On many manors this office was attached only to the larger holdings, as their tenants were more likely to possess the authority to exercise it.[110] It would seem that the Thaxted reeve was democratically elected by the bondmen, but how his office was executed and which of the tenants tended to be most regularly chosen remain unknown.

The surviving records tell no more of the office of hayward, but no doubt his duties and responsibilities were similar to those defined in *Seneschaucie*.[111]

The reeve and hayward appear to have been the only elective offices at Thaxted. As already seen,[112] the duties of parker, keeper of the gates of the parks and swineherd were attached to specific freeholds. If there were other offices, such as beadle, then these were presumably the lord's appointments, as no mention of them is found.

The call of the lord upon a bondman's time did not end with the performance of labour services and the liability for manorial office. As often as once in every three weeks the bondman (and the freeholder)[113] might have to make his suit of court (i.e. appear at the lord's court). Examination of the medieval court rolls of many Essex manors shows that the ancient duty of suit of court 'from three weeks to three weeks' rarely, if ever, was demanded, because there was insufficient business to warrant it. The manor of Thaxted was, however, sufficiently populous for this often theoretical duty to be a near reality,[114] at least in the latter half of the 14th century, for which alone there is evidence. In the year 1361-2 eleven courts, in 1377-8 sixteen courts, and in 1380-1 thirteen courts were held.[115]

[109] See H. S. Bennett, *op. cit.*, pp. 168-178, for an excellent account of the office of reeve.

[110] *Ibid.*, p. 169.

[111] *Walter of Henley's Husbandry, together with an anonymous Husbandry, Seneschaucie, etc.* ed. E. Lamond. (Royal Historical Society, 1890).

[112] See p. 11.

[113] Although the Partition of 1348 and the Survey of 1396 do not assign to a number of freeholders and a few bondmen suit of court, this is, of course, no evidence that they were exempt from the duty.

[114] Another example is the manor of Writtle. See MS. court rolls from 1379 in E.R.O. (D/DP M178 *et seq*).

[115] See pp. 70, 82, 95.

III

THE FOURTEENTH CENTURY—
AGE OF GROWTH AND RADICAL CHANGE

The development of a considerable urban nucleus about the manor house and the church by the middle of the 14th century has already been briefly mentioned.[1] In 1348 the town contained 90 houses and 36 shops.[2] How far this growth had been brought about by settlement of cutlers in the manor or whether they only hastened the process during the course of the century will probably never be known. A good deal has been written about the cutlery industry in Thaxted, but it is extremely difficult to separate tradition from truth. The work of some writers who are possibly quoting facts is rendered useless by their failure to cite references and by the mixture of fact with undoubted legend.[3] The 1348 Survey (Partition)[4] and the 1393 Survey[5] lend no support to the presence of a sizeable cutlery industry. The former assigns a trade to only one tenant—a smith—though the surnames 'Coteller' and 'Schether' are found; the latter describes two tenants as sheathers but none as cutler and the surname 'Haftere' occurs.

There is, however, one document which gives a firm basis for the unsupported testimony of previous writers on Thaxted. It is a Poll Tax Return, undated but ascribable to the year 1381.[6] While it is notorious that these particular returns were greatly falsified,[7] a study of the Thaxted return in relation to the 1393 Survey gives good grounds for the belief that it was falsified chiefly, if not solely, by the almost total omission of spinsters and widows.[8] Of the 249 males listed, no less than 79 are described as cutlers and 4 as sheathers; in addition there were 11 smiths and 2 goldsmiths, a number of whom were doubtless working wholly or partly for the cutlery trade. Over one-third of the listed adult male population was thus engaged in this one industry. Precisely when the cutlers settled in the town remains conjectural, but it seems unlikely to have been much before the early years of the 14th century when the borough was created.[9] By the middle of the century the industry was well established, for 4 of the 79 cutlers in 1381 are identifiable with tenants in the 1348 Survey (Partition) and the families of another 18 were in the town at that date. As a number of the cutlers in the Poll Tax

[1] See p. 8.

[2] The 1348 Survey (Partition) actually gives 35½ shops. 'Shop' may here mean either a place for the sale of goods or a workshop.

[3] e.g., Rev. J. E. Symond, 'Thaxted and its Cutlers Guild', in the *Transactions* of the Essex Archaeological Society, Vol. III (New Series, 1889); Ethel M. Simcoe, *Thaxted* (Saffron Walden, 1934).

[4] *C.C.R.*, 1345-1348, pp. 525-540.

[5] See pp. 33-66.

[6] P.R.O., E.179/107/49.

[7] See, for instance, Sir Charles Oman, *The Peasants' Revolt* (1906); C. M. Beresford, 'The Poll Tax Returns of 1377, 1379 and 1381', in *The Amateur Historian*, Vol. 3, No. 7, 1959, pp. 271-278.

[8] The total of 416 individuals listed is made up of 166 married couples and 84 single persons, of whom but one is a woman.

[9] See p. 22.

Return were not manorial tenants, but leased dwellings and shops in whole or in part from others who were, the figures of 4 and 18 are minimal.[10]

From the holdings of the 38 tenants in the 1393 Survey who appear as cutlers in the Poll Tax Return, it is found that their dwellings and shops were chiefly located in the main street[11] and in Middle Row.[12] Indeed the number of messuages and shops in the latter occupied by cutlers suggests that their coming to the town may have led to its development as a housing site, at a time when expansion elsewhere, convenient to water supply, would have been difficult.[13]

To the question 'Why did so many cutlers settle at Thaxted ?', the surviving records offer no reply ; nor may a satisfactory solution be found elsewhere. There were no local sources of iron, and the metal must therefore have been brought considerable distances. True, there was a plentiful supply of wood in the district for smelting and for the making of the hafts of knives, though this was no less true of many Essex towns and villages. On the further question ' Where did the cutlers find markets for their products ? ', the record is equally silent. As the only substantial centre of the industry in the county it may be assumed that they were found in many an Essex market and fair, but whether Thaxted cutlery found its way to London or to other distant places remains unknown. It is tempting to see in the four merchants named in the Poll Tax Return, evidence of some marketing organisation for the cutlery.

In addition to the cutlers and smiths a large number of other crafts and trades were represented in the town in 1381, as shown in the following table, though most must have served purely local demand.

Craft or Trade	*No. engaged*	*Craft or Trade*	*No. engaged*
Cutler	79	Merchant	4
Smith	11	Draper	1
Sheather	4	Tailor	10
Goldsmith	2	Cooper	1
Carpenter	6	Brewer	11
Turner	1	Butcher	3
Tiler	4	Baker	2
Box or Basket-maker	3	Poulterer	1
Barker (Tanner)	3	Fishmonger	1
Cordwainer	1	Carter	4
' Soutere ' (Cobbler)	1	' Pedder ' (Pedlar)	1
Pelter	1		155[14]

[10] A comparison of the Poll Tax Return and the 1393 Survey shows that of 38 cutlers identifiable in the latter 3 were holding only purprestures or small parcels of land. A number of these of course may have had their dwellings and shops in the other quarter part of the manor.

[11] i.e., ' Margreteswell ' to ' Shepecotelane ' and ' Chaloneresbrigge ' to ' Hallgate ' in the Survey. See sketch map III.

[12] See sketch map III.

[13] See also p. 27.

[14] Of the remaining 95 names, 41 are designated labourer ; 1, shearman ; 1, parker ; 1, drover ; 12, ' frank ' tenants ; 9, bond tenants. A further 15 have no description and 15 cannot be given any status owing to defects in the document.

In the 14th century a structure of industry arose in which a large proportion of the tenants of Thaxted found employment, thus divorcing them from the essentially agricultural organisation of the manor. At some date prior to 1348, and probably early in the century, the lord of the manor must have recognised this economic fact, but whether willingly or unwillingly and at what price is unknown. Henceforth many inhabitants of the town were described as burgesses (*burgenses*) and the area of the manor within which they dwelt as a borough (*burgus*). Although legally within the manor, the borough became administratively a separate entity.[15] The free tenants living outside the borough become termed as *liberi tenentes forenses*,[16] to distinguish them from the burgesses living in the town, but it is not location of dwelling alone that distinguishes the one from the other ; indeed, in some cases, as will be seen shortly, this may be no distinction at all. Unlike the freeholder, the burgess, according to the 1393 Survey, was not bound to do suit to the lord's court from three weeks to three weeks, but only once in the year after Easter in addition to attendance at the leet held after Michaelmas ; he rendered only a money rent for his burgage ; and from among his own number he elected, presumably each year, a chief representative—the bailiff of the borough—the symbol of corporateness implicit in the term 'burgus'[17] and of independence from the rest of the manor.

The independence thus won, however, did not extend to any real measure of self-government, as the continued necessity to attend the lord's court once a year and the annual leet shows. Municipal self-government had to await the granting of the Charter of Incorporation by the Crown in 1556.[18] Papers in a dispute between the lord of the manor and borough of Thaxted and the recently created Charter borough heard in the Court of Wards and Liveries in 1562 indicate that the bailiff of the borough had by the reign of Henry VIII attained the title of mayor.[19] He never sat to keep court, however, 'but was of courtesy, called thereto by the lord's steward and then paid of old custom threepence for his "cusshinge" as often as he sat with the steward at the lord's court in Thaxted'.[20] In Thaxted, whatever it might mean in other towns,[21] borough status in the 14th century meant only considerable freedom from manorial obligations but no conferment of municipal responsibility. At most, the burgesses had obtained some measure of control of the weekly market and the two annual fairs, paying a fixed farm of 4s. 4d. yearly for the stalls in the market and compounding for the tolls at markets and fairs by an annual payment of 5s.[22]

Territorially the borough did not take in the whole of the urban centre, nor even a compact area within it. In the same street a house held by a *burgens* might lie sandwiched between two dwellings occupied by *liberi*

[15] It will be observed that in the 1393 Survey (pp. 33-66), the *burgenses* are given at the end, after the rents and services of the other tenants have been summarised.

[16] See p. 40.

[17] See p. 59. These attributes of burgage tenure are only ascribed to the first burgess listed in the 1393 Survey, but obviously apply to the others.

[18] *C.P.R.*, 1555-1557, pp. 154-156 ; D/DHu T29.

[19] D/DHu T30/4.

[20] D/DHu T30/5.

[21] See J. Tait, *The Medieval English Borough* (Manchester, 1936), especially pp. 206-213.

[22] See p. 65.

tenentes ; a *liberus tenens* might have *burgenses* as neighbours on either side ; and both might abut on a town house held by one of the other sub-manors in the parish. No hint of this is given in the 1348 Survey (Partition), but may be strongly suspected from that of 1393. For in it both freeholders and burgesses hold dwellings in Park Street, in the main street between 'Margareteswell' and 'Shepecotelane' and in the lane itself.[23] As no abuttals are given, however, this suspicion may only be made a certainty by detailed examination of the much more comprehensive surveys of the manor and borough made in the 16th and 17th centuries.[24] On the plan[25] plotted from their evidence, the extent of this division between the manor of Thaxted, the borough and the other sub-manors of the town properties may be seen. Although by the 16th century the town had grown still further and some changes in the manorial structure may have taken place,[26] the later surveys still reflect the divisions between burgage and freehold tenures which obtained in the 14th century. This complexity may be explained by the fact that the seignorial borough at Thaxted in the 14th century had no rights of self-government, which would have necessitated a unified, easily defined area over which the burgesses could have had jurisdiction. The absence of defined burghal limits was to be a material cause of the long dissension between borough and lord in the 16th century after the grant of charter.[27]

Much of the structure and organisation of the agricultural manor of Thaxted, as distinct from its 'burgus', described above, did not survive the 14th century, except as a legal concept which economic forces had robbed of any basis in reality. The presence of a flourishing township within the manor must have been something of a disturbing influence ; and on that unknown day when the lord granted burgage rights in the township, giving enhanced freedom to many of its inhabitants, he undoubtedly helped to undermine the old manorial order.

The 1348 Partition[28] offers little evidence of any change in the manorial organisation which has been outlined. As far as can be ascertained, there was no commutation of labour services at that date, though the summary arrangement of the record reduces its value as complete evidence of this. Only a small proportion of the demesne in the open arable fields[29] and one small piece of demesne meadow[30] were leased to tenants at will, in no way suggestive that the working of the home farm for the direct benefit of the lord was coming to an end. More significantly, certain tenants' holdings which had fallen into the lord's hands by escheat or upon failure of heirs had been regranted to new tenants, not in return for rents and services, but for a fixed money rent.[31] This freed them from bond services, but they had not the security of tenure which was afforded to those who were still liable to carry out all the old obligations. The latter held at the will of the lord, but according to the custom of the manor—a real measure of protection. The tenants

[23] See pp. 41, 42-43, 59-60, 63.
[24] D/DHu M22-34 ; see also list of primary sources at end, p. 103.
[25] See sketch map III.
[26] e.g., Coldhams Fee appears to have been created after the 14th century.
[27] See p. 22.
[28] *C.C.R.* 1346-1349, pp. 535-540.
[29] *Ibid.*, pp. 526, 535, 537, 538.
[30] *Ibid.*, p. 535.
[31] *Ibid.*, pp. 527, 532, 535, 538 ; see also p. 66.

of the escheated and heirless lands were holding by lease at the will of the lord. The basis of their tenure had in effect lost its manorial character.

It is only possible to identify the original tenure of two holdings held as leaseholds at will in 1348 : a virgate called 'Puntes',[32] and 'Rollescoescroft'[33] which had been a freehold messuage and curtilage. The former status of 'Duketteslond'[34] and 'Paunfylonyslond'[35] is unknown. In the one instance where a comparison may be made, the leasehold rent of the virgate called 'Puntes' given at 30s. in 1348[36] was less than the total value (32s. 8¾d.) of the rents and services of a similar virgate then still held customarily.[37]

None of the evidence of the 1348 Partition considered in isolation can, however, be taken as symptomatic of the economic break-up of the manor. All the peculiarities which have just been noticed may have had special causes. It is only when they are considered in relation to an analysis of the *compoti* of 1361-2, 1377-8 and 1380-1,[38] and finally the Survey of 1393,[39] that they gain a greater significance. By the date of the first compotus, 4 half-virgaters' holdings, an 'akermanslond' and a 'coterellond' had fallen into the hand of the lord of the manor[40] and were now held by tenants as leaseholds. Sixteen years later a further 2 half-virgates, 2½ 'akermanslonds' and 3 'cotterellonds' were being similarly held. By 1381 the tenure of two further 'cotterellonds' had been similarly converted. On the eve of the Peasants' Revolt, fundamental changes had already occurred in Thaxted. Summarised, the tenurial division of bond holdings at that date was thus :

Tenurial status	*Still held by rents and services*	*Held at farm*
Molmen	All holdings, *but see p. 14*	—
Virgaters and Half-Virgaters	3¾ virgates	4 virgates
Akermen	5½ 'akermanlonds'	3½ 'akermanlonds'
Coterells	7 'coterellonds'	4 'coterellonds'
Cotmen	6 'cotmanlonds'	—

A significant number of bondmen had thus become detached from the ancient tenurial structure and economic organisation of the manor. But the break-up of the economic organisation was even more advanced than the tenurial changes might suggest. An increasing amount of the demesne was also being leased for terms of years. In 1348 only a little over 47 of the 1160

[32] See p. 54.
[33] See p. 66.
[34] See pp. 40, 66.
[35] See pp. 39, 66.
[36] *C.C.R.*, 1346-1349, pp. 527, 532, 535, 538.
[37] *Ibid.*, p. 535.
[38] See pp. 67-102.
[39] See pp. 33-66.
[40] Isabel daughter of Edward III who on the death of William de Bohun Earl of Northampton was granted the wardship of three parts of the manor which had come to the inheritance of Edmund Earl of March, then a minor (see p. 4), and the wardship of the remaining fourth part during the minority of Robert Tibetot, *C.P.R.*, 1358-1361, pp. 532-3.

acres of demesne in the open fields was at farm, in five parcels widely varying in size, and 1¼ acres of demesne meadow.[41] A slightly reduced acreage of leased demesne arable (45¼ acres) is shown in the *compotus* of 1361-2 under the heading 'Farm of Lands'.[42] There follows, however, the heading 'New Farms' [of demesne]. Unfortunately only the total income from this source is given, £24. 3s. 9d., without any details of the acreage thus leased. By comparison with the yield from the 45¼ acres of arable and 1¼ acres of meadow recorded under 'Farms of Lands'—23s. 10d.—a very considerable proportion of the demesne was by then leased away. But this cannot be used precisely as an index to the actual acreage, for a chance misplaced entry in the *compoti* of 1377-8 and 1380-1 suggests that the 'new farms', at least where a large parcel of land was concerned, were leased at a lower rent per acre. In them the lease of 159 acres of demesne in 'Northfeld' was incorrectly included under 'Farm of Lands' instead of 'New Farms' of demesne[43] and the rent given was 23s. 6d., averaging a little over 1¾d. per acre. Having regard to this undoubtedly very low figure, it seems probable that over half the demesne arable, meadow and pasture was leased by 1362, when the 'new farms', as has been mentioned, brought in rents totalling £24. 3s. 9d.[44] By 1378 this total had increased to £37. 0s. 1d.[45] and to £41. 8s. 0d. in 1381.[46] These increases must be attributed solely to further leases of demesne, for the individual rents of 'old' farms of demesne show no upward trend between 1362 and 1381, though there is some variation in the rents of escheated or heirless bond holdings held by lease.[47] Whether or not the 1381 figure of £41. 8s. 0d. indicates that the whole of the demesne arable was by then leased to tenants, this was so by 1393.[48]

The working of any of the arable for the lord had ended by 1362. The *compotus* for that year has no account of its produce; the virgaters and half-virgaters performed no ploughing service[49]; and no bondman was called upon to work in the great open fields in winter,[50] to tend their crops during the summer or to harvest them in the autumn.[51] Never again at Thaxted would the reeve and hayward[52] be called upon to organise the unfree peasantry to perform their 'bederippes' or prepare their 'bedeacres' ready for the cart. Only some of the demesne meadow continued to be mown for the lord by customary works. In 1362 this amounted to less than half the total acreage, 42¾ out of 95¼ acres[58]; by 1378 only 17 acres of hay were thus made[54] and in 1381 a little more, just over 18 acres.[55]

In 1361-2, however, the remaining pool of customary labour still had its use to the lord in an emergency. In the winter of that year a storm struck Thaxted causing much damage: the two windmills were 'thrown down' and

[41] Survey (Partition), 1348, *C.C.R.*, 1346-1349, pp. 526, 535, 537, 538.
[42] 45¼ acres of arable and 1¼ acres of meadow. Only the parcel of meadow is identifiable with those parcels given in the 1348 Survey (Partition).
[43] See pp. 81, 94.
[44] See p. 69.
[45] See p. 82.
[46] See p. 94.
[47] See pp. 39, 40, 54.
[48] See p. 34.
[49] See p. 73.
[50] See p. 74.
[51] See pp. 74-75.
[52] The hayward was still receiving a wage in 1362, but not in 1378 or 1381.
[53] See p. 76.
[54] See p. 88.
[55] See p. 102.

the grange destroyed[56]; many roofs were stripped and other buildings about the manor were wrecked; fences were blown down and hedges damaged.[57] A good deal had essentially to be done by skilled paid labour, such as tiling and rebuilding the mills,[58] but bond tenants on whom the burden of winter works still lay were called upon to rebuild the grange, make roofs secure and repair the fence and hedges about the great park (' Southfrith ') and ' le Parkmade '.[59] In 1378 the customary works of these same tenants were again called upon to renew the hedge about the Great Park. When Thaxted suffered a further storm accompanied by flooding in May 1381, however, no customary labour services were called upon: all repairs were undertaken by paid craftsmen and labourers,[60] except for some voluntary help rendered by ' divers men ' who were rewarded for their assistance.[61] In that year even hedges and fences were renewed by paid labour.[62]

At least as early as 1361, therefore, the disintegration of the old manorial order was almost complete. The demesne in the sense of a home farm was no more: the arable not yet in the hands of leasehold tenants was derelict, being worked neither by customary nor paid labour, and the pasture was all sold away, for the lord no longer had any livestock of his own; only part of the meadow was yielding him produce direct. Apart from hay, the demesne could only offer timber from the parks for sale[63] and agistment for beasts there.[64] Except upon the extraordinary occasions mentioned there was consequently no need for customary labour, and labour services not already commuted were sold away.[65] As already seen, by 1381 such services were not exacted even in an emergency.

The manor now had in practice, if not entirely in theory, a purely money economy.[66] The Survey of 1393[67] shows that, for the three-quarters of the manor which it represents, the fundamental changes which have been traced had then reached their logical end—all the demesne had been leased and all bond tenants were holding their dwellings and lands ' at farm '.[68] The elaborate description of the services to be rendered by the tenants was still legally valid but economically—and so in reality—already a dead letter.

The progress of the 14th century witnessed a steady growth of the township, which was to accelerate quite considerably in its last two decades or so. The Survey (Partition) of 1348[69] records 78½ dwellings held by burgage

[56] See pp. 71, 74.
[57] See pp. 71, 74.
[58] See p. 71.
[59] See p. 74.
[60] See pp. 96-97 for the interesting items of the account for the repair of bridges, the two windmills, etc.
[61] See p. 97.
[62] See p. 97.
[63] See p. 69.
[64] See p. 69.
[65] See pp. 73-75.
[66] It will be seen from the *compotus* for 1361-2, pp. 67-77, that all rents in kind had been commuted for money payment, as had the render of corn and multure from the farm of the two mills.
[67] See pp. 33-66.
[68] It will be seen that in the Survey (pp. 48-53) the molmen are not shown to be holding their lands at farm with commuted services. It was unnecessary to do so, for by the peculiar features of their bond tenure they had in effect long enjoyed the freedom from labour services lately won by the other bondmen, except upon exceptional demand (see p. 14).
[69] *C.C.R.*, 1346-1349, pp. 525-540.

tenure; in 1393 the three-quarters of the manor represented in the Survey below[70] alone had 88 houses held in burgage. A rental of 1405-7 relating solely to the burgage tenements[71] lists 113, an increase of nearly 44 per cent. over the 1348 total. The borough rents steadily grew during the century, with a more rapid increase after 1381.

Rents of the Borough
(exclusive of farm of stalls and market tolls)

1348	1362[72]	1378[73]	1381[74]	1405-7
£4. 9s. 6½d.	£5. 2s. 2¾d.	£5. 6s. 11¼d.	£5. 7s. 10¾d.	£8. 14s. 3¾d.[75]

None of these progressive increases was due to a raising of individual rents, which remained stable throughout; they are attributable solely to the increase of burgage holdings in the town.

Before 1348 there were no doubt vacant plots in the streets of the town where new houses might at any time have been built, but extensive development along one side of the main thoroughfare, in Bolford Street and Park Street,[76] became possible only when the site of the manor house, its yards, courts and gardens were granted to tenants in parcels after the Partition. There was similarly an increase in the grants of small plots of land on the fringes of the open fields, where they met the backsides of the houses or the highway. Some of these plots were no doubt retained by tenants to form gardens or extensions of gardens, but others were undoubtedly used as sites for new houses. The surviving *compoti* show increases in 'new' rents of the borough from these sources and from purprestures in the main street and Middle Row. In 1362 there were 19 'new' rents[77]; this total had increased to 41 in 1378[78] and 46 in 1381.[79] The 1393 Survey[80] and the Rental of 1405-7[81] show that this process continued into the 15th century. Nor does the figure of 19 'new' rents in 1362 reflect the whole growth of borough rents since 1348, for exclusive of 'new' rents the total of these had risen from £4. 9s. 6½d. to £4. 13s. 3d. in that period.

How long this expansion continued into the 15th century is outside the scope of this study, but certainly it had ceased by the 16th century. Indeed, the town was already seriously declining, even 'in great ruin and decay', to quote the words of the royal charter of incorporation[82] which it obtained in 1556. It is ironical that Thaxted should have obtained the ultimate goal of progress to municipal self-government in a fruitless attempt to avoid economic decay. This is borne out by a Survey of 1593[83] which records only 73 houses

[70] See pp. 59-65.
[71] E.R.O., D/DHu M18.
[72] See p. 67.
[73] See p. 79.
[74] See p. 91.
[75] In 1393 the rents from three quarters of the borough totalled £5 1s. 3¼d. (see pp. 59-65); in 1348 they had been £3 4s. 6¾d. (*C.C.R.*, 1346-1349, pp. 525-540); by 1405-7 they had risen to £7 9s. 6d. (E.R.O., D/DHu M18).
[76] See sketch map III.
[77] See pp. 67-68.
[78] See pp. 79-81.
[79] See pp. 91-93.
[80] See pp. 59-65.
[81] E.R.O., D/DHu M18.
[82] *C.P.R.*, 1555-1557, pp. 154-6.
[83] E.R.O., D/DHu M23a.

held by burgage tenure and rents totalling £3. 18s. 8¼d., less than half the figure for 1405-7. The fall in the number of houses in the later surveys possibly explains the houses whose manorial ownership could not be established in preparing Map III: they may have been largely decayed burgage or free rents of the manor of Thaxted.

The destruction of the old economic order is also reflected in the distribution of the various tenures among the population in 1393 as compared with in 1348. Since, by the latter date, the lord received only a monetary return (except suit to his court) for a holding of any tenure, there was no economic disincentive to a freeholder seeking the tenancy of a bond tenement, other than a rent higher than he had been accustomed to pay in virtue of the commuted services. A single individual holding by more than one tenure was certainly not unknown in 1348, as is seen in the table below, but it was much more common by the end of the century. There is a marked increase in the numbers of tenants holding by both free and bond tenures.

	1348[84]	*1393*
Holding by burgage tenure only	62	76
Holding by free tenure only	59	37
Holding by bond tenure only	49	28
Holding by lease[85] only	—	2
Holding by mixed tenures, viz.		
Free and burgage	10	20
Free and lease	—	5
Free and bond	1	11
Free, burgage and lease	2	—
Free, burgage and bond	1	4
Free, bond and lease	—	3
Burgage and bond	2	3
Burgage and lease	2	1
Bond and lease	2	—

Any social distinction between the free and the bond tenant which had once existed could not survive these changes. Henceforth social status would be determined far more by the amount of land owned than by the nature of its tenures, whatever lawyers and their treatises might say for centuries to come. For the freeholder, profitability would be the determining factor in his decision to seek the tenancy of a bond holding. If it was conveniently near his free lands and had good soil, if the rent including the value of the commuted labour services was not too high, its bond tenure would be no great discouragement.

An analysis of all the bond holdings and of freeholdings of three acres and above in the three parts of the manor in 1393 and in 1348 shows a tendency for the size of a family's holding to increase. Of the twenty-one families

[84] The 1348 figures are based on an analysis of the purparties of Margery de Roos, Maud de Veer and Elizabeth de Bohun in the Partition (*C.C.R.*, 1346-1349, pp. 525-540) only, the same three parts of the manor as are represented in the 1393 Survey (pp. 33-66).

[85] i.e. lease of demesne or of escheated or heirless lands.

holding identical lands in 1393 as in 1348, eleven had increased the size of their holdings, seven were the same and only three held less land by the later date.[86] Most noteworthy was the growth of the lands held by the Godard and Setarde families. In 1348 John Godard was holding a virgate at farm and a half virgate and four acres of land in bondage; in 1393 a John Godard (probably the former's son) no longer held the four acres, but had in addition another half virgate, a molman cottage and seven acres, and a half interest with Nicholas Setarde in the Despenser (formerly Tiptoft) fourth part of the manor, which Robert Hethe, the steward, was holding to their use. He had also had possession, with four others, of another half virgate, but this was probably only as a trustee. Even more remarkable is the expansion of the Setarde holdings, which in 1348 consisted only of a cottage and one acre held by John Setarde. Nicholas Setarde in 1393 was tenant of this tiny cotman holding, but he had also an acre of free land and an acre of free meadow, was joint tenant of a free messuage and eight acres of land, and with John Godard had the joint interest in the Despenser fourth part of the manor. He, too, was one of the five tenants, probably as a trustee, of the half virgate. This apparent success story of the 14th century must be qualified with the reservation that John Setarde in 1348 may have been something more than the humblest of bondmen, for he may have had lands in another adjoining manor.

The changes in the distribution of tenures among the population, the increases or decreases in the extent of lands held by a particular family, all point to mobility in the transfer of land. But only a close analysis of the two Surveys of 1348 and 1393 shows how great that mobility was, once the economic shackles of the old manorial order had been thrown off. The results of such analysis are incorporated in the table below. From them it is seen

Tenure	No. of Holdings in 1393 Survey	In same family in 1393 as in 1348	Partly in same family, partly in another 1348 family	Partly in same family, partly in a non-1348 family	In another 1348 family	In a non-1348 family	Partly in another 1348 family, partly in a non-1348 family
Freeholders	82[87]	17	—	—	33	31	1
Molmen	28	6	1	1	11	8	1
Virgaters & Half-Virgaters	12	4	1	—	4	3	—
Akermen	5	2	—	—	2	—	1
Coterells	6	2	—	—	3	1	—
Cotmen	4	3	—	—	—	1	—
	137	34	2	1	53	44	3

that slightly less than a quarter (24.82 p.c.) of both free and bond holdings, were still in the same family in 1393 as in 1348. Dividing the holdings into

[86] See *sub. nom.* (H)abraham, B(i)enge, Boyton, Ewayn, Godard, Hanecok, Hardy, H(i)erde, Ilger, FitzRauf Richemond, Setarde, Terry, Thrower, Underwode, Wodeward in Partition, 1348 (*C.C.R.*, 1346-1349 pp. 525-540), *sub* Roos, Veer and Bohun purparties, and in Survey, 1393, below.

[87] This figure disregards purprestures and similar tiny holdings of land.

free and bond, the percentage for the former is 20.73 and for the latter 30.9, a difference that is scarcely great. Of the holdings which had passed into other hands, 38.67 p.c.[88] were now in the hands of families whose names are in the 1348 Survey, and, more significantly,[89] 32.12 p.c.[90] were in the tenancy of families whose names do not figure among the manorial population in 1348. A small number of holdings (1 free and 4 bond) were held jointly by combinations of these family groupings.

A similar analysis of burgage holdings cannot be made, for their nature (baldly described as 'a messuage' or 'a shop') and the form of the 1348 Survey (Partition) do not permit positive identification of a burgage at both dates; nor is the number of burgages static, but is considerably increased.[91] There is ample evidence, however, that there was as great or even greater mobility in the rate of transfers of burgages in the fact that almost six out of ten (59.09 p.c.) of burgage messuages in 1393 were held by tenants whose family names are not in the 1348 Partition. Slightly over half the shops (52.38 p.c.) were also in the hands of such newcomers.

Conclusion

It only remains to see how the picture of Thaxted that has been drawn fits into the canvas of 14th century history—or better, into the wider canvases of that century, for in the past twenty years radically different interpretations of the later medieval period have been put forth, particularly in regard to economic and demographic trends. The older school of thought saw the 14th and 15th centuries as a period during which the upward trend in population and economic wealth of the 13th century was generally continued, and considered the effects of the Black Death and the subsequent visitations of plague in 1361 and 1369 as temporary, though serious, upsets to this trend.[92] The more recent hypothesis is that, on the contrary, the later medieval period was under the shadows of declining population and contracting agriculture and industry.[93]

Of these two opposed generalisations, the history of Thaxted in the 14th century as developed above clearly accords with the older theory and indeed presents a picture of expansion to a degree which none of its protagonists would claim as being typical of the country as a whole.[94] Of the effect of the Black Death, the catastrophic nature of which is accepted by historians,

[88] 40.44 p.c. of free holdings, 36.36 p.c. of bond holdings.

[89] See also p. 31.

[90] 37.81 p.c. of free holdings, 23.64 p.c. of bond holdings.

[91] See p. 27.

[92] See for example J. E. Thorold Rogers, *Six Centuries of Work and Wages* (1909), pp. 222 *et seq*; and J. H. Clapham, *A Concise Economic History of Britain* (Cambridge, 1949); also F. M. Page, *The Estates of Crowland Abbey: A Study in Manorial Organisation* (Cambridge, 1934).

[93] For a review of both sides of the argument and further evidence in support of the newer hypothesis, see M. Postan, 'Some Economic Evidence of Declining Population in the Later Middle Ages', in *The Economic History Review*, Second Series, Vol. II, No. 3 (1950), and works cited therein.

[94] For a recent examination of the growth of the cloth industry in the Stroud Valley in the 15th century, see E. M. Carus-Wilson, 'Evidences of Industrial Growth On Some Fifteenth-Century Manors', in *The Economic History Review*, Second Series, Vol. XII, No. 2 (1959).

though the duration of its effects is much argued, there is no documentary evidence for Thaxted. At most, it can be said that if the incidence of mortality were anywhere near the computed national average, the level of population had recovered and even slightly increased by 1362.[95] Such recovery and increase must have been due to an influx of population.[96] Colour is lent to this possibility by the fact that only 56 of 138 family names found in 1393 are traceable in the 1348 Partition. The upward trend in population continued throughout the remainder of the century, unaffected noticeably by any further visitations of pestilence. Although there is little information about the trade and industries of the town in this period, the increase of population and house building[97] indicate a parallel growth in prosperity.[98]

It is in the context of an expanding urban population and the fundamental changes which had taken place in Thaxted that the spread of the Peasants' Revolt there must be considered.[99] What was it that made the men of Thaxted, in common with the tenants of so many other Essex manors, descend upon the manor house and burn the court rolls and other evidences? As the *compotus* of 1380-1 shows, no labour services were being exacted, and they had been demanded only at time of emergency at least since 1361; an ever-increasing number of holdings was being held at farm; the demesne was no longer being worked by the lord, who was therefore not competing for labour with the richer peasants[100]; there was clearly no great bar in practice to an individual tenant holding land by both free and bond tenure. All or some of these factors applied on many other manors to which the Revolt spread. On the face of it, there would appear less reason for the Revolt to have spread to Thaxted than to many other Essex manors.

But if the economic grievances of the Thaxted tenants were not so manifold as elsewhere, their feelings of social and legal injustice were no less. They could not foresee that the tide of history was running in their favour, but lived in a state of continual uncertainty whether the lord of the manor would some day turn back the clock and assert his undoubted legal rights over them. Because they had tasted freedom as a result of the dissolution of the old economic order, they wished that freedom to have the sanction of the law. It was no accident that the abolition of bondage was the first point in the demands of the peasants gathered at Mile End. Thus it was that at Thaxted too the evidences of inferior status were destroyed. Unfortunately for them some detailed record, perhaps kept outside the manor, must have survived, on which the status of all the tenants and the customs declared in the 1393 Survey were based. The apparent attempt of the tenants to concoct a

[95] See p. 27.

[96] For future examples of rapid recovery, see A. Levett, *Black Death on the Estates of the Bishopric of Winchester* (Oxford Studies in Legal and Social History, Vol. V. Oxford, 1916).

[97] See p. 27.

[98] It is perhaps no accident that the most splendid of ecclesiastical monuments in Essex, the parish church of Thaxted, was largely built in this century.

[99] See p. 58. As far as is known this reference to 'tempore rebellionis' in the 1393 Survey is the only evidence that the Revolt spread thither.

[100] On this matter of competition between the lord still farming the demesne and the richer peasant, see R. H. Hilton, 'Peasant Movements in England before 1381' in *The Economic History Review* Second Series, Vol. II, No. 2 (1949).

custumal of their own (?after the failure of the rebellion) was in vain.[101] The note in the 1393 Survey concerning the revolt indicates that the issue and the antagonism were still very much alive, accentuated, not diminished, by the continued break-up of the old economic order.

Of the role of the burgage tenants, pursuing the cutlery or some other craft, with little or no direct interest in the agriculture of the manor, nothing is known. No doubt, in such an expanding community, active in trade and crafts, there was generally a considerable demand for the available supply of labour, and the operation of the Ordinance and Statute of Labourers aroused discontent in both employers and employed at the curb put upon wages and mobility of labour.[102] The independent attitude of the burgesses towards the lord may also be seen in the 1393 Survey, where a number of them are said not to be paying rents (mainly in respect of purprestures) 'because he does not agree with the steward about the same'.[103] If these burgesses played no part in the actual revolt, they were a constant example to the bondman of the status and dignity before the Law which he was seeking for himself.

The foregoing study of the manor of Thaxted in the 14th century does not by itself add any decisive weight to a particular school of thought on this transitional period. It is clear, however, that until a far wider sample of the vast store of manorial and borough records which have survived so remarkably[104] is published and analysed, many statements made by earlier historians will be questioned and the work of those who question them will remain based at least partly on hypothesis and conjecture. It was as a small contribution towards this end that this study was begun.

[101] See p. 58.
[102] R. H. Hilton, *op. cit.*
[103] See p. 62.
[104] The medieval records of a large number of manors housed in the Essex Record Office have hardly been touched by scholars, despite their accessibility.

SURVEY OF THREE FOURTH PARTS OF THE MANOR OF THAXTED, 1393

[*Thax*[1]]*stede*

Whereas on the fourth day of Dece[mber in the[1]] twenty-first [year of the reign[1]] of King Edward the third from the Conquest of England the manor there was divided into four parts among [the heirs[1]] of Giles de Baldelesmere, that is to say, Margery, wife of William de Roos of Hamelak'[2], Maud, wife of John de Veer' [Earl[1]] of Oxford, Elizabeth, wife of William de Bohun, Earl of Northampton, & John Tiptoft at that time in the custody [of the lord King[1]] by reason of his minority; and three parts of the manor aforesaid, that is to say, the purparties of the aforesaid Margery, Maud & Elizabeth [*several words illegible*[3]] lord Earl of March by reason of the death of Elizabeth Countess of Northampton, his mother [*several words illegible*[3]] March who lately died enfeoffed certain persons in the manor aforesaid, that is to say, Richard le Scrop' [*some names illegible*[3]], knights, John Bisshopeston', Walter de Colmpton' & Hugh de Boraston [*some names or words illegible*[3]] desiring to know clearly what and how many commodities or profits appertain to the same manor [*several words illegible*[3]] by making evident what sort and kind &c. And therefore by the inquisition held there before the said Robert [on the tenth day of May[4]] in the sixteenth [year[4]] [of the reign of King Richard the second[1]], it was presented that there appertain to the same manor, as to three parts [aforesaid, the site of the manor[4]] [*several words illegible*[3]] the several arable lands, meadows & pastures, two windmills, the rents & services of [the free tenants, bond tenants[4]] [*several words illegible*[3]] burgesses, the rents & services of the same, fairs and markets, three parks, that is to say, 'Oldefrith'' ['Southfrith'' & 'Lytel'[4]] [Park[1]] [*several words illegible*] declaration of [all[1]] & singular was made hereafter. And because mention was not made in the aforesaid partition of [how long the perch was[4]] by which the lands, meadows, pastures and parks were measured, it is declared that the perch by which now &c. contains in length five 'Taille Yerdes' and five inches. And after all these things have been declared other evidences will appear whether &c., that is to say, what kind of liberties appertain to this manor & the tenors of the charter by which &c.

Firstly, there is a certain site of the manor there in which are the houses next to and above the outer gate with all the grange now standing for receiving the lord's council and for holding courts, in addition to those houses which are demised to farm as within, which are valued yearly after deduction 6s. 8d.; and there are in the same manor other houses in the lower court, that is to say, various ruined rooms which are worth nothing yearly after deduction, because they are not repaired. And the aforesaid site containing three parts of the manor contains, that is to say, in 'Bolefordegardyn' 11 acres and it is not valued annually by the acre, because it is demised as a whole with other parcels of land as will appear within. And the purparty of Tiptoft, that is to say, **3 acres 3 roods 9 perches**[5] abutting towards the middle of 'la Burton'. And in 'le Countessegardyn' 5 acres 1 rood 15¼ perches and it is not valued by the acre for the aforesaid reason. And the purparty Tiptoft there next 'les Hilles', **2 acres 1½ roods 18¾ perches.** And in 'le Burton' 1 acre 1½ roods 5¾ perches. And the purparty of Tiptoft there **1½ roods**. And there are in the same 'le Berneyarde', 'le Vttercourt', 'le Innercourt' with the way to 'le litelparkgate' and 'le Pounfolde'. And thus is the sum of all the acres within the manor except the acres demised in fee to divers tenants as within appears

17 acres, 3 roods, 1 perch

[1] Documents mutilated: letters and words in brackets supplied.

[2] Where extension of a name is doubtful or impossible abbreviation is retained and marked by an apostrophe.

[3] The words are obliterated by a large ink-stain.

[4] The words in brackets may only be read with the aid of ultra-violet light.

[5] Figures and words set in bold type are underlined in the original. The scribe thus indicates amounts which are not to be reckoned in the total; but it will be seen that he did not observe this convention of medieval accountancy with regularity.

And be it remembered that Lord Philip Spencer, 'Chivaler'', who in the right of his wife holds a quarter part of the manor formerly assigned to John Tiptoft, has free ingress and egress [*about three words illegible*] purparty of the places, where the houses of his purparty have been built and to his gardens which are being worked, with easement and 'Poundefolde' at his will, as appears by the partition made among the aforesaid heirs on the aforesaid fourth day of December in the twenty-first year of King Edward the third returned in the Chancery of the Lord the King. But Robert Heth', now steward of the lord, has taken this quarter part to farm to the use of John Godard' and Nicholas Cetard' for them and theirs paying therefore yearly to the same Philip [*blank*].

And there were there the arable and several lands lying in three 'seasons'[1], that is to say, 'North'feld' with 'Worthe', 'Boxstede' with 'Newefelde', 'Asshefelde', while the lands were worked by the lord, but now they are demised to farm. And the 'seasons' are made at the will of the farmers.

Firstly of the 'season' of 'North'felde' with 'Worthe'

Roos

37 acres 3½ roods and 15 perches in one piece of land abutting on 'Smalmade' at one head and extending towards the mill.

8 acres ½ rood in one piece next 'Millepath'' on the north part and abutting on the meadow of Ralph son of Ralph.

16 acres ½ rood and 6 perches in one piece of land extending from 'Smalmade' unto 'Stunkewillemade' on the east part of one piece of land assigned to John Veer', Earl of Oxford.

8 acres 3 roods 7 perches in one parcel abutting on the pasture of John Bienge at the west head either side of 'le Chircheway'.

Veer'

33 acres ½ rood 7½ perches in the same field in one piece next 'Glouerslane', extending from the meadow of Robert Cartere unto 'North'mell''.

29 acres 1½ roods and 4½ perches in the same field in one piece next the hedge of Adam Henr' and William Hardy and extending at one head on 'Smalmade' and at the other head on 'Stunkewellemad''.

7½ acres ½ rood and 13 perches in the same field in one piece lying on 'Bulford-hulle' next land of John, son and heir of John Tiptoft'.

4 acres 3 roods 7 perches in one piece there on 'Rihulle' abutting on the river bank towards the east.

4 acres 3 roods 16 perches in one piece there next land of Thomas May abutting on 'Raescroft' towards the east.

Bohun

33 acres 1½ roods there in 2 pieces whereof the first lies next 'Coldehamhegge' and the other abuts on the meadow of John Bienge from 'Abramford'', in which there is a 'Meere'.

5 acres 3 roods and 16 perches in one piece there abutting on 'Wepyngshot'' at one head and the other on the meadow of Ralph FitzRalph.

23 acres 3 roods and 16 perches in one piece there lying on 'Rihull'' next the purparty of Margery de Roos between 'Smalmade' and 'Stunkewellemad''.

12 acres 17 perches in one piece there lying on 'Chirchehull'' next the croft of Andrew Bienge and the greenway towards the meadow on the south part.

8½ acres ½ rood and 19 perches in one piece there abutting on 'Abrambrugge' lying next 'Hungrewill'' on the north part.

[1] Refers to the three-field system, whereby one field was sown with winter crops, the second with spring crops and the third lay fallow. In Thaxted the winter crop was apparently wheat and the spring crop oats when the demesne had been worked for the lord (see p. 74).

Roos

10 acres 3½ roods in addition to 1 acre 18 perches demised to John Legate and in addition 1 acre 3 roods demised to John Brugge in fee.

Sum — 249 acres 3 roods 4 perches. And now this land is measured by John Godard' and John Throwere, junior. And there is found as an increase by their measurement — 8 acres ½ rood and 2¾ perches.

And there remains to Lord Philip Spencer' 83 acres 3½ roods 4 perches in the field of 'Northfelde'.

And there remains to the feoffees there — 257 acres 3½ roods 6¾ perches.

Of the 'season' of 'Asshefelde'

Roos

13½ acres 10½ perches in the field of 'Asshefelde' in one piece of land there which is according to the measurement next a piece of land assigned to John, son and heir of Margaret, who was wife of John Tiptoft.

19½ acres ½ rood 10 perches in one piece of fallow land next 'Oldefrith'', abutting on 'Shepecotemade' towards the north part.

77 acres 1½ roods 18½ perches in one piece there in which is contained 'le Wodwille' extending towards 'Shepecotemade' at the southern head, towards 'Boitonhegge' towards the north. [N. Homffrye *added in margin in a later hand*].

Veer'

30 acres 3½ roods and 16 perches on the fourth measurement there.

22 acres 7½ perches in another piece of fallow and arable land at the south head of land of Earl of Northampton and Elizabeth his wife.

42½ acres 6 perches in one piece there on the east part of the road called 'Berdefeldendewy', extending towards 'Boiton'hegge' towards the north.

15 acres 7 perches in one piece there called 'le Tonge' between 'Shepcotemade' on the south part and 1 piece of meadow called 'Golpeshyrne', lying between land of the said John, son and heir of John Tiptoft, and land of Earl of Northampton and Elizabeth his wife.

Bohun

27 acres 1 rood 11 perches as the bounds there show, lying next the purparty of the said Earl of Oxford and Matilda on the north part.

30½ acres ½ rood 11½ perches as well of fallow lands as of arable lands in 1 piece there abutting on 'Shepecotemade' at the north part.

47 acres 3½ roods 10½ perches in one piece lying between 'Boitonmore' and 'Golpesherne' towards the west.

4 acres 16 perches are there in one piece called 'le Tunge' at 'Golpesherne'.

Sum — **331 acres 1½ roods 4 perches.** And now by the measurers aforesaid no increase is found, because it is strict measure etc.

And there remains to Lord Philip Spencer' in the same field **111 acres 3 perches.**

And there remains to the feoffees in the said 'season' — 331 acres 1½ roods and 4 perches.

Of the 'Season' of 'Boxstede' with 'Newefeld'

Roos

40 acres in the field of 'Boxstede' in one piece of land between the east side of the field of the Prior of Stok' and a boundary towards the east, on the north part [*of*] 'le longemere', together with a piece of land between the way from 'Vicariescroft' called 'le Nook'' and a piece, which John le Clerk' holds at farm at will of the lord, containing **13 acres** and 3 roods, with one piece of land next 'Prioriscroft' extending by the road next 'Mikeline' towards 'Fromondecroft'.

14 acres and 4 perches in the same field in one piece of land next 'Maresschallhegge', whereof one head abuts on 'Longeboxstede' and the other on land of Thomas Dessex'.

6 acres of land there in one piece of land called 'Fromondescroft'.

3½ acres 5 perches in one piece there of 'Milleschot' between land assigned to Earl of Northampton and land assigned to the Earl of Oxford.

Veer'

42 acres in one piece which extends as far as 'Plompton'more' on one side and the other side next 'Fromondiscroft' extends on land of Margery de Roos, with one piece lying between 'Plomptonemore' and 'Hobekenyscroft', containing in all [*blank*].

8 acres and 18 perches in one piece next land of Nicholas Gile on the north part and abuts on the croft of William atte Lane towards the west.

12 acres 10½ perches in one piece lying in 'Longeboxstede' on the east part.

1 acre 1½ roods 1 perch in one piece on the east part of 'Milleschot' next 'Milleway', abutting on land of the Prior of Stoke. [Note for 'milleway' *added in margin in a later hand*].

Bohun

40 acres 3 roods 16 perches in a certain piece in 'Boxstede', lying next land of John Richemond'.

13 acres 10½ perches in one piece in 'Longeboxstede' lying next 'Milleway' on the east part. [Note for 'milleway' *added in margin in a later hand*].

5½ acres ½ rood 1½ perches in two pieces which Margery de Essex' holds at farm at will, whereof one is enclosed with hedge. [Note this *added in margin in a later hand*].

4 acres 1 rood and 1 perch as the metes and bounds there show in one piece of 'Milneshot', lying between the part of Margery de Roos, the part of John, son and heir of John Tiptoft, and abutting on the mill-pond.

Roos

13½ acres ½ rood and 16½ perches in the field called 'Newefeld'' in one piece of land lying there next land of Richard Loksmyth'.

1½ acres ½ rood 4½ perches in the same field in one piece of land which William Drught holds at farm.

9½ acres 13 perches in the same field in one piece of land which the vicar of 'Thaxstede' holds at farm at will of the lord.

Veer'

13 acres ½ rood 7 perches lying in one piece at the entrance of 'Newefeld'' next 'Shepecotebrugge'.

11 acres and 6 perches lying in one piece called 'Pedderescroft'.

Bohun

6 acres 3½ roods 11½ perches lying in one piece of 'Newefelde' next land of Richard Loksmyth' and Richard Virly.

4 acres ½ rood 5½ perches in one piece there lying between land of the said Richard Loksmyth' and 'le Longehegge'.

13 acres ½ rood and 9 perches in one piece of 'Newefeld'' next land of John Cousyn'.

Sum — **264 acres 1½ roods ½ perch.** And now by the measurers aforesaid there is found an increase in 'Boxstede'. Total **10 acres 2 roods 16¼ perches.**

And there remains to Lord Philip Spencer' there **63 acres 2 roods 9 perches.** And also there are found in 'Newefeld'' by way of increase **1 acre ½ rood 3½ perches.**

And there remains to Lord Philip Spencer' **26 acres 1 rood 15 perches.**

And there remains to the aforesaid feoffees Lords of this manor — 276 acres ½ rood ¼ perch.

Sum of all the acres of arable lands of the demesne abovesaid 865 acres 1½ roods 11 perches and to P[hilip] Spenser' **284 acres 3 roods 15 perches.**

Parkmade

Roos 8 acres 1 rood 18 perches there next the highway.

Veer' 8 acres ½ rood 11 perches there next the fence on the south part.

Bohun 8 acres ½ rood 9 perches there next the purparty of Veer' on the north part.

Sum — 24 acres 2½ roods 18 perches. And by the measurement of the aforesaid there is an increase of a ½ rood; nevertheless, it is not counted, because all the feoffees to the same meadow mow the appurtenances.

And there remains to Lord Philip Spenser' **8 acres ½ rood.** And to the feoffees

Sum — 24 acres 2½ roods 18 perches.

Pamfilonnesmade

Roos 1 acre ½ rood 2 perches there next the hedge of Walter atte Fenne.

Veer 1 acre ½ rood 2 perches there next 'Rytherwykesmede'.

Bohun 1 acre ½ rood 2 perches there next the purparty of Veer'.

Sum — 3 acres 1½ roods 6 perches. And there is nothing in excess, but there remains to Lord P[hilip] Spenser' there 1 acre ½ rood 2 perches. And to the feoffees

Sum — 3 acres 1½ roods 6 perches.

Brodefenne

Roos 1 acre 1 rood 2 perches there called 'Milleacre'.

1 acre 3½ roods 4¾ perches next the meadow of Thomas Roger'.

Veer' 2½ acres ½ rood 3¼ perches next the meadow of the aforesaid Thomas.

2 roods 3½ perches next the same meadow.

Bohun 1 acre ½ rood 19 perches called 'Heuedacre'.

1 acre 3½ roods 7¾ perches next the hedge of John Blake.

Sum — **9 acres 2¼ roods.** And there is in excess ½ rood 19¾ perches.

And there remains to Lord Philip Spenser' **3 acres ½ rood 6¾ perches.** And to the feoffees

Sum — 9 acres 3 roods.

Shepecotemade

Roos 4 acres 3 roods 1½ perches there next 'Oldefrith''.

Veer' 4 acres ½ rood 10½ perches there called 'Golpeshirne'.

2 acres 3 roods there next the purparty of Bohun.

Bohun 5 acres 1 rood 13¼ perches there.

Sum — **17 acres 5¼ perches.** And there is an increase of **1½ roods 14¾ perches.**

And there remains to Lord Philip Spenser' **6 acres 2 roods 18¾ perches.** And to the feoffees

Sum — 17 acres 2 roods.

North'made with Stunkwelmade & Smalmade

Roos 7 acres 10 perches in one piece there on the north part of 'Petesbrugg''.

3½ roods 8½ perches there abutting on 'Oldehamhegge'.

1½ acres next 'Ilgeresmede', abutting on the croft of John Gile.

Veer' 6 acres 3 roods 18 perches there next the meadow of Nicholas Gile.

2¼ acres 12 perches there next the demesne meadow.

Bohun 6 acres 1 rood 2¾ perches next the meadow of May & 'Abramesbrigge'.

1 acre 1 rood there in the tenure of John Benge at farm.

2 acres ½ rood 7 perches in 'Smalemade' next the meadow of Ralph filtz Rauf'.

Sum — **28 acres 2 roods 18¼ perches**; and now by the aforesaid measurement there is found an increase of **1 rood 10 perches.** And there remains to Lord Philip Spenser in 'North'mede' & 'Stunkewellemede' **9 acres 1½ roods 13½ perches.** And there remains to the feoffees there

Total — 28 acres 3½ roods 8¼ perches.

Sum of all acres of meadow — 84 acres 1 rood 12¼ perches. And to P[hilip] Spenser **28 acres 2 roods 1 perch.**

Stotteslese

Roos 7 acres 3 roods in one piece next 'Bolfordmade'.

Veer' 6 acres 3 roods abutting on 'Serlebrigge'.

Bohun 6 acres 3 roods 2 perches there on either side of 'le logge'.

There is no increase, but there remains there to Lord Philip Spencer' **6 acres 3 roods.** And to the feoffees

Sum — 21 acres 1 rood 2 perches.

Hilles

Roos 7 acres ½ rood 5 perches on the south side of 'Bolfordgardyn'.

Veer' 7½ acres ½ rood 5 perches on the south side.

Bohun 7½ acres ½ rood 5 perches.

There is no increase, but there remains there to Lord Philip Spencer' **7½ acres ½ rood 5 perches.** And to the feoffees

Sum — 22 acres 1½ roods 15 perches.

Busshes

Roos 5½ acres 14 perches next the highway.

Veer' 6 acres 3 roods 5 perches abutting on 'Wynthereswell''.

Bohun 5½ acres 14 perches next the demesne pasture.

There is no increase, but there remains there to Lord Philip Spencer' **5½ acres 14 perches.** And to the feoffees

Sum — 17 acres 3½ roods 13 perches.

Sum of all acres of pasture — 61 acres 2½ roods 11 perches. And to Philip Spencer' 19 acres 3½ roods 19 perches.

Litelpark'

Roos 40 acres on either side of 'le heuthegge'.

Veer' 41 acres 3½ roods 9½ perches on the west side of 'le Ouerhewt' next land formerly of William Richmond'.

Bohun 40 acres 6½ perches next 'Gaymhaphegge'.

There is no increase, but there remains to Lord Philip Spencer' **40 acres.** And to the feoffees

Sum — 121 acres 3½ roods 16 perches.

South'frith' alias the greate park

Roos 13½ acres between 'Palmershewt' & 'Ferthynghewet' & abuts on 'ChufferESwell''.

64 acres 3½ roods 2 perches there called 'busshewey'.

59 acres 1½ roods 4 perches called 'Hankokesquarter''.

27 acres 3½ roods on the east part of 'Hancokesquarter''.

Veer' 19½ acres 7 perches called 'Palmershawt' next 'Palmershegge'.

91 acres 3 roods 14 perches called 'Dame Imaygneshewt'.

29½ acres ½ rood 18¾ perches in 'Godardeshawt' next 'Ferthyngeshawt'.

Bohun 7½ acres in 'Palmershewt' on the north part of Veer'.

89½ acres called 'Hobekonyshowt''.
50 acres 3 roods 2 perches on the Lodge.

21 acres 1½ roods 19 perches in 'Hermyteshewt' on the south side of 'Heremeteshok', abutting on the wood of the Abbot of Colchester.

There is no increase because it is strictly measured and nevertheless twice is measured, but almost the whole park is oak-timber of the age of 60 years, and the underwood there grows badly controlled. And there remains to Lord Philip Spencer' 165 acres 2 roods 13½ perches. And to the feoffees

Sum — 506 acres 1 rood 16¼ perches.

Oldefrith'

Roos 44 acres 3 roods in one piece next the holding of John Hawley.

Veer' 44 acres 3 roods in one piece next Roos.

Bohun 14 [*sic*][1] acres 3 roods in one piece next the holding of Thomas Tendrynge.

No increase but there remains there to Lord Philip Spencer **44 acres 3 roods**; and to the feoffees of 'Sesonablewod''

Sum — 134 acres 1 rood.

Sum of all acres of wood — 762 acres 2 roods 12 perches. And to P[hilip] Spencer 250 acres 1 rood 13½ perches.

Pannfiloneslond'

And memorandum of 'Pannfiloneslonde' containing 23 acres 3 roods 16 perches of arable land & 1 acre 2½ roods of meadow, formerly demised to Edmund Daniell' for **16s.** annually, and is now demised to Henry Munde for **12s.** as appears within, receiving three parts of the farm or three parts of the land at will of the lord, that is to say **9s.**

[1] Should read '44 acres'.

Pounteslond'

And memorandum of 'Pounteslond'' containing 27½ acres ½ rood 9 perches of arable land & 3 acres of meadow, formerly demised to John Godard', bondman, for **30s.** annually, and now is demised to John Godard' for 20s. as within, receiving **15s.**

Duketeslond'

And also of 'Duketeslond' containing 41 acres ½ rood 8 perches of arable land demised to Nicholas Richemond' as appears within, receiving 3 parts of the said land or farm of **18s.**

Mills

And there are there 2 windmills, whereof one is called 'North'Mille' & the other 'Chirchemylle', whereof the lord shall have three parts of the farm as appears within and shall meet 3 parts of the cost for the reason above specified.

Now of the Foreign Free Tenants Paying at the Terms of

	Christmas	Easter	Nativity of John the Baptist	Michaelmas
Bulfordestret				
John Bateman holds 2 acres of land, paying yearly[1]	5d. 2 capons	5d.	5d.	5d.
John Thomasson Venour holds one piece of land next 'Bulfordesgardyn' near 'Bulfordbrigge', in length 100 feet & in width 28, & pays	1d.	1d.	1d.	1d.
Wykerestrete				
John Elmeswell & William Richerfeld' hold one cottage & pay yearly	1d.	1d.	1d.	1d.
William son of William Wymbussh' holds one acre of meadow called 'Okelondemade'	9d.	9d.	9d.	9d.
Thomas Rogerson' Wymbussh' holds one purpresture at the end of his garden in 'North'felde', in length 35 feet & in width 8 feet, & pays yearly	—	—	—	1d.
William son of William Wymbussh' holds one purpresture at the end of his garden in 'North'feld'', in length 32 feet & in width 15, & pays yearly	—	—	—	1d.
Thomas son of William Wymbussh' holds one purpresture at the end of his garden in 'North'feld'', in length 32 feet and in width 15	—	—	—	1d.
John Dix holds one purpresture next to his garden in 'North'felde', in length 19 feet & in width 12 feet	—	—	—	1d.
William Clerevaux holds one purpresture outside his garden, in length 40 feet & in width 10, & pays yearly	—	—	—	1d.
Andrew Neel holds one postern gate for pedestrians outside his garden towards 'North'feld'' & pays yearly	—	—	—	1d.

[1] 'Widow H' added in margin in a later hand.

William Asshele holds one purpresture in 'North'felde' next his garden, in length 50 feet & in width 7	—	—	—	1d.
John Sauston' holds one purpresture in 'North'feld'' next his garden, in length 30 feet & width 7	—	—	—	1d.
John Brigge, 'shether', holds one purpresture in 'North'felde' next his messuage, in length 30 feet & in width 7 feet, & pays yearly	—	—	—	1d.
William Asshele holds 9 perches of land in 'North'feld'', as appears in the court held 27 day of September in the fifteenth year of King Richard the second, & pays yearly	—	1½d.	—	1½d.
William son of William Wymbussh' holds 9 perches of land, as appears in the same court, & pays	—	1½d.	—	1½d.
Thomas son of William Wymbussh' holds 12 perches there, as appears in the same court, & pays	—	2d.	—	2d.
John Dix the elder holds 20 perches there, as appears in the same	—	3¼d.	—	3¼d.
William Clarevaux holds 20 perches there, as appears in the aforesaid court, & pays yearly	—	3¼d.	—	3½d.
Thomas son of Roger Wymbussh' holds 77 perches there, as appears in the same court, & pays yearly	—	12d.	—	12d.
Thomas Wygor' holds 30 perches there, as appears in the same court, & pays yearly	—	5d.	—	5d.
John Brugge, 'Shether', holds 137 perches there, as appears in the same court, & pays	—	23d.	—	23d.
The same John holds there 2 acres 6 perches, as appears in the aforesaid court, & pays yearly	—	2s. 4¼d.	—	2s. 4¼d.

Newefelde

John Kent holds one house there next 'Shepecotbrigge'	—	9d.	—	9d.

Fro Wekerescroft to Margreteswelle

John Benge holds one messuage formerly of Nicholas atte Hyd'	3d.	3d.	3d.	3d.
Thomas Warwyk' holds one messuage, 2 acres of land 3 roods	2¼d.	2¼d.	2¼d.	2¼d.
John Sparowe holds one purpresture & pays yearly	¼d.	—	—	—
William Asshele holds one purpresture & pays	¼d.	—	—	—
Edward Lamberde holds one purpresture & pays	¼d.	—	—	—
John Copcy holds one piece in 'Lorimerscroft'	¼d.	—	—	—

Fro Margreteswell' to Shepecoteslane

Richard Skilman holds 12 acres of land in 'Wodham' & pays	6d. 1 capon	6d.	6d.	6d.
Thomas Thrower', Thomas Warwyk' & associates hold a tenement sometime Russell's	2½d.	2½d.	2½d.	2½d.
Thomas May holds 9 acres of land in 'litell' Asshefelde' & pays yearly	4¾d.	4¾d.	4¾d.	4¾d.

Fro Kentesbrigge to Assh'felde fote Wey

Nicholas Herlyng' holds one purpresture & pays	½d.	½d.	½d.	½d.
Walter Wakeleyn holds one purpresture & pays	1d.	1d.	1d.	1d.
The same Walter holds one purpresture & pays	1d.	1d.	1d.	1d.
John Kent holds one purpresture next to the tenement formerly of John Shether' & pays yearly	—	—	—	½d.
John Fox & John Essex' hold 2 purprestures & pay	1¼d.	1¼d.	1¼d.	1¼d.

Fro litelbrigge to Berdefeldendeward to Millehacch'

John Chamberleyn holds one messuage & half an acre of land, will make suit of court from 3 weeks to three &c., & pays	2¼d.	2¼d.	2¼d.	2¼d.
John Bataille holds one messuage & 1 acre of land & pays	7½d.	7½d.	7½d.	7½d.
John Godloue holds one messuage with appurtenances & pays	4¼d.	4¼d.	4¼d.	4¼d.
John Copcy holds 3 roods of land & pays	—	4½d.	—	4½d.

Fro litelbrugge to Setardescorner'

John Osekyn holds one messuage with appurtenances & pays	7d.	7d.	7d.	7d.
Nicholas Cetard' holds one acre of freeland purchased of Bartholomew Chamberleyn & gives as an increase	—	—	—	½d.
The same holds one acre of free meadow purchased of Thomas Bray & pays yearly	—	—	—	½d.

Parkestrete[1]

John Brigge, John Fox & others hold one messuage, one acre of land with appurtenances & pay yearly	3d.	3d.	3d.	3d.
The same John & John hold one acre 3 roods of land with appurtenances in 'Worth'' & pay	8d.	8¾d.	8¾d.	8d.
John Legat holds one acre 18 perches of the same 'Worth'' & pays yearly	4½d.	4½d.	4½d.	4½d.

[1] Only the first three entries of this section are bracketed in the original under 'Parkestrete'.

Thomas May & Nicholas Setard' hold one messuage, 8 acres of land with appurtenances, will make common suit	2s.	2s.	2s.	2s.
The same hold one purpresture opposite their house	½d.	½d.	½d.	½d.
Simon Sauard' holds one cottage containing 1 acre of the tenement which Thomas Wodewarde holds	1d.	1d.	1d.	1d.
John Blunt holds 2 acres of land & pays	2d.	2d.	2d.	2d.
John Pipere holds 2 pightles & pays	½d. 1 capon	½d.	½d.	½d.
Robert Auenant holds one messuage, 1 acre 1 rood of land & 1 purpresture & pays yearly	1d.	1d.	1d.	1d.
John Alman, 'Barker'', holds one purpresture there	—	½d.	—	½d.
John Clerk' holds one croft called 'Gunyldcroft'' & pays by the year at the feast of Saint Botolph 2 ploughshares worth 14d. & pays	2¼d.	2¼d.	2¼d. 2 ploughshares	2¼d.
'Augnes' Hawkyn holds one acre of land & pays	1½d.	1½d.	1½d.	1½d.
Joan Stace holds one messuage, 1 acre of land & pays	2½d.	2½d.	2½d.	2½d.
John Hadstoke holds one messuage, 1 acre and a half of land & pays	4½d.	4½d.	4½d.	4½d.
John Venour holds one messuage, 6 acres of land, will make suit of court from 3 weeks to 3 weeks & pays	14¾d. 3 capons	14¾d.	14¾d.	14¾d.
John Hadstoke holds 2 acres of land & pays yearly	6d.	6d.	6d.	6d.
John Williem holds 3 roods of land & pays	¾d.	¾d.	¾d.	¾d.
John Richemond' the elder holds 1 acre of land, formerly of John atte Gate	1¾d.	1¾d.	1¾d.	1¾d.
John Saward' holds [*blank*] of land formerly his father's	2½d.	2½d.	2½d.	2½d.
Thomas Hyrd' holds one messuage & pays yearly	2 capons			

Know present & future that I Richard of Clare Earl of Gloucester and Hertford have granted & by this my present charter confirmed to Bartholomew, the parker of Thaxstede, twenty-four acres of arable land with appurtenances & two acres of meadow in the town of Thaxstede, & pasture for sixteen cattle in my great park of Thaxstede and for twelve pigs during the whole year, except the month of breeding of the beasts, & housebote for three houses, that is to say, the hall, the grange and the byre, & haybote for his court in the said park which is called 'South'Frith'' & reasonable firing of dead wood as well as of greenwood by the view, nevertheless, of the bailiff of the place in the aforenamed park. And be it known that, if any cattle or any pig beyond the aforesaid number granted and confirmed in this writing to the aforesaid Bartholomew be found in the oft-mentioned park, it is to be taken without claim by him or his heirs as property to the use of me or of my heirs. I have granted also to the same & confirmed from any dead beast taken in the aforesaid park & the other two smaller parks one shoulder & for a live beast given one penny to be received from the donor; to have & to hold all the aforesaid as is aforesaid to the same Bartholomew & his heirs freely & quietly by hereditary right for ever of me & my heirs by the service of serjeanty of keeping the aforesaid three parks of Thaxstede, so that nevertheless, I and my heirs shall be allowed to assart and cut the underwood throughout the places in the said great park and to enclose; [*and*] neither the said Bartholomew nor his heirs may claim no [*sic*] common in those assarts or enclosures. And that all the aforesaid may possess the power of perpetual strength, I have caused my seal to be affixed to the present writing. These being witnesses, Lord William de Wauton', Lord Roger son of Bartholomew, Lord John de Essex, Lord John Bansard', Richard de Beucondr', Walter Forestar' &c.

Keepers of the gates of the parks

John Richemond', the elder, holds one messuage & one acre of land, and will shut and open the gate of the park of 'South'-fryth'' there and will make the hedge of the park during the whole year, receiving of the lord for each perch **1d.** and old wood, & pays no rent

John Serle holds one messuage & one acre of land within 'Litelpark'' & will close & open the gate of the same park next his house well and efficiently; and if anyone shall have strayed from the way in the park by night, he will lead him back safely; and he will repair the palings during the whole year in the manner following: that if they shall make the paling anew the lord will have the wood felled and will carry it to the place to be made and he [*John Serle*] will cut and make [*the palings*] receiving of the lord for each perch **1d.**; and any week he will perambulate the park, and if he shall come upon faults in the fence he will repair, that is to say, that if he put one or two new palings in a perch, he is to take nothing of the lord nor of the park, but if he renew more than two in one perch or in divers perches he will receive of the lord for 3 perches **1d.**, and he will make anew when it shall be necessary; he will repair the hedges around the said park, taking for his labour the old hedge, & gives no rent.

William Hubert holds one messuage & 3 acres of pasture within the said park, doing in everything as John Serle and gives no rent; but be it remembered that this William has nothing except a messuage both for a 'Coterellond'' and for making this service.

Richemondes grene

John Richemond' the younger holds one messuage with 80 acres of land & 2 acres of meadow by keeping the 3 parks of the lord according to the tenor of the charter.

The same[1] holds 2 acres of pasture called 'Wyntereswell'' (2s.) & one croft called 'Dame Imaigne croft' (6d.) next 'South'frith'', 1 pightle called 'hopkyneshamstall'', one messuage (6d.) called 'Stephenes' with one croft of 4 acres, 12 acres next 'South'frith'' called 'Bussheceroftes' (4s. 6d.), one acre newly built on next 'vikerestrete' (6d.), certain lands in Coldham (6d.), one piece of ground (2 capons) on which Walter Baker' dwells, one meadow called 'Plumpton' Moore' (2 hens, 4 geese), and certain other lands (12d.)

2s. 5½d.	2s. 5½d.	2s. 5½d.	2s. 5½d.
2 hens	2 capons		4 geese

[1] 'Bur' added in margin in a later hand.

which, by his confession on the making of this [*survey*], at present he does not know; and he will make common suit and pays				
Nicholas Richemond' for one purpresture opposite his tenement	—	—	—	½d.
John Abram holds one purpresture there & pays	—	—	—	½d.
John Colman holds one purpresture there & pays	—	½d.	—	½d.
William Whiteloue holds one purpresture & pays	—	—	—	½d.
Monkestrete				
John Kent holds one acre and a half of meadow & pasture & pays	3d.	3d.	3d.	3d.
John Clerc holds certain tenements as his own as Thomas May & Robert Hubert formerly held of the said John, & pays	6d.	6d.	6d.	6d.
The same John holds 2 parcels of pasture purchased of John Saucer' & John Brigge, & pays yearly	2d.	2¼d.	2d.	2¼d.
The same John holds one rood of meadow sometime Wygot's & pays	½d.	½d.	½d.	½d.
The same John holds one purpresture against the messuage of John Smertman & pays yearly	½d.	½d.	½d.	½d.
And the same John owes suit of court from 3 weeks to three for 3 roods of meadow sometime of John Man				
Joan Venour holds one purpresture at 'Okhall' & pays	1½d.	1½d.	1½d.	1½d.
The Abbot of 'Tilthey' holds one messuage, 60 acres of land & meadow, will make common suit and pays yearly	12d.	12d.	12d.	12d.
Akermanstrete				
John Auenant holds one toft, 5 acres of land & pays	4d.	4d.	4d.	4d.
John Abraham, 'tyler'', holds one purpresture & pays	¼d.	¼d.	¼d.	¼d.
Westwode				
Walter Russhede holds 'Pounstonmade' & pays	1d.	1d.	1d.	1d.
Nicholas Saucer' holds land formerly [*blank*] & pays	5d.	5d.	5d.	5d.
William Saucer'[1] for one acre and a half of land & pays	1¼d.	1¼d.	1¼d.	1¼d.
Nicholas Richemond'[2] holds one messuage, 71 acres of land & meadow, will make common suit & pays yearly	—	3s. 6d.	—	3s. 6d.

[1] 'Overall' added in margin in a later hand.

[2] 'Key' added in margin in a later hand.

The same Nicholas[1] holds 12 acres purchased of Thomas Rauf' & 12 purchased of his father & will make suit	14¾d.	14¾d.	14¾d.	14¾d.
John Palmere holds 2 acres of land and pays	2d.	2d.	2d.	2d.
John Pycot holds one acre of land	2¾d.	2¾d.	2¾d.	2¾d.
John Badewey holds one purpresture	—	½d.	—	½d.
Nicholas Richemond'[1] holds 5 acres of land & pays	3½d.	3½d.	3½d.	3½d.
William Ilger' holds 2 acres of land in Coldham & pays	2d.	2d.	2d.	2d.

Bieucotelersgrene

The same William holds one messuage, one acre of land	1d.	1d.	1d.	1d.
Sybil Clemere holds one messuage & one acre of land & pays	¾d.	¾d.	¾d.	¾d.
Joan Colle holds 2 acres of land & pays yearly	3¼d.	3¼d.	3¼d.	3¼d.
William Ilger' holds 12 acres of land & pays yearly	2s. 6d.	2s. 6d.	2s. 6d.	2s. 6d.
Thomas Ewayn[1] holds one messuage & 9 acres of land	6d.	6d.	6d.	6d.
Walter Ewyan [*sic*] holds one messuage & 3 acres of land	3d.	3d.	3d.	3d.
John Adamson Herry holds one croft & 1 piece of meadow of 'Horell'' & pays yearly	7d.	7d.	7d.	7d.
Joan Colle holds 2 acres of land formerly of Richard Saucer' & pays	1½d.	1½d.	1½d.	1½d.
The same holds one piece of land formerly of J. Hirde of Westwod'	—	½d.	—	½d.

Wodham

Margaret fitz Rauf'[2] holds one messuage, 60 acres of land, will make suit of court from 3 weeks to 3 & pays yearly	—	2s. 10d.	—	2s. 10d. 1 lb. cumin
The same Margaret holds 18 acres of land of the tenement 'Jemes' & owes common suit and pays	16½d.	16½d.	16½d.	16½d.
William Hirde holds one messuage, 20 acres of land & 1 acre of meadow and will keep the lord's swine during the year, receiving of the lord & [*blank*] & his rent quit; & if he does not keep [*the swine*] he pays yearly as &c'. & makes common suit	12d.	12d.	12d.	12d.
The same William holds 2 acres of land & pays yearly	3d.	3d.	3d.	3d.

[1] 'Bull' added in margin in a later hand.

[2] 'Jeremye Key' added in margin in a later hand.

Richard Wakeleyn holds one messuage, 3 acres of land & will make common suit and pays yearly	7d.	7d.	7d.	7d.
John Bienge holds 4 acres of land of the tenement 'James' and owes common suit [*for*] the whole tenement	3d.	3d.	3d.	3d.
Thomas Tewe[1] holds 6 acres of pasture and makes common suit & pays by the year	—	—	—	1d.
The same John Benge [*sic*] holds one grove formerly of Roger atte Welde & pays yearly	—	1½d.	—	1½d.
William Yerdele holds one messuage & one acre of land	4d.	4d.	4d.	4d.
John Proude holds 4 acres of land of the tenement 'James', which same tenement owes common suit, & he pays yearly	4d.	4d.	4d.	4d.
Henry Boyton' holds one messuage & 30 acres of land, meadow & pasture & owes common suit & pays	—	15s.	—	15s.
The same Henry holds half a virgate of land of the tenement sometime of Golsmyth' & owes common suit and will make 3 services of carrying corn and hay, receiving of the lord **4½d.**, or will give to the lord **6d.**, & pays yearly	20¼d.	20¼d.	20¼d.	20¼d.
William Symond' holds 3 acres of land & pays yearly	4½d. 1 capon	4½d.	4½d.	4½d.
Thomas Maij holds 6 acres of land & one purpresture & pays	4¼d.	4¼d.	4¼d.	4¼d.
Walter Ewayn holds 6 acres of land & 1 piece of meadow & pays	2¼d.	2¼d.	2¼d.	2¼d.
John Herry, 'bocher', holds 1 acre of land & pays	1d.	1d.	1d.	1d.
John Thrower', John Dod' hold one acre of land & pay yearly	1d.	1d.	1d.	1d.
John Stelewomman holds half acre of land in little 'Asshefelde' formerly purchased of John son of Richard Godard', bondman, as an increase & pays yearly	—	—	—	½d.
William Symond' holds 2 acres of land & pays	—	1½d.	—	1½d.
John Godard' holds 1½ roods of free land & gives on account of the increase	—	—	—	¼d.

Fro Millehach' to Prioureshall'

John Aleyn holds one messuage with curtilage and pays yearly	4½d.	4½d.	4½d.	4½d.

Hauerhille

Agnes Cok' holds one toft with one house & pays	—	—	—	1d.
John Cobbe & Richard atte Thorne hold one acre of land there & pay yearly	—	3½d.	—	3½d.

[1] 'Salmon' added in margin in a later hand.

John Godefrey holds certain lands there & pays	—	3½d.	—	3½d.

To be discharged

Of **2d.** formerly issuing out of the parcel formerly of Richard Daubere in 'Wykerestrete', or of **2s. 2d.** issuing out of one messuage with curtilage formerly of 'Rulleco' there, or of **2s. 2d.** issuing out of 1½ acres of land formerly of John Bally between 'Millehach'' & 'Prioureshall'', nothing, because they fell to the lord by escheat and have been demised among the farmers as within

Shepecotelane

John Kent holds one messuage there towards 'Newefelde' next the brook, containing one rood, & pays	4½d.	4½d.	4½d.	4½d.
[*Totals*]	31s. 5½d.	69s. 5¼d.	31s. 3¾d.	70s. 9¼d.
	13 capons	—	2 plough-shares	4 geese
	2 hens	—	—	1 lb. cumin

Sum 10 li. 2s. 11¾d.

Item from 3 services of carrying hay & corn without deduction 6d.

Now of the bond-tenants called Moolemen

Thomas Bolter' & Agnes Spryngold' hold one messuage & one virgate of land, and will plough for winter seed 3 acres, for Lenten seed 3 acres, and for fallow-land 3 acres, receiving of the lord for each acre **3d.** And thus this plough-service is worth after receipt, in that the ploughing of the acre is worth **8d.,** 3s. 9d. And they will carry with one cart with 2 horses and men for three days, that is to say, for one day hay, for 1 day wheat, for 1 day oats or pease, receiving of the lord for this carrying service **9d.,** each day 3d. And it is worth after receipt 2s. 6d. And they will work with the lord in Autumn for 8 days called 'bederipdayes', receiving of the lord for each day one loaf, whereof 10 are made from one bushel of wheat, & everyday cheese to the value of **¾d.** & pottage. And this 'bederippe' is worth after deduction 2s. And they will prepare for the cart one 'bedeacre', receiving of the lord 2 loaves of the measure aforesaid, & this 'bedeacre' is worth after receipt **6d.**; and they will be hayward if etc., and not reeve, will not give heriot, will make common suit, & pay to the lord yearly	21d.	21d.	21d.	21d.

Berdefeldende

Thomas Wodward', John Frenssh', John Richemond', the elder, hold one messuage, half a virgate of land and will carry with 1 cart with 2 horses [*and*] 2 men hay for a half a day, wheat for a half day, oats or pease for a half day, receiving of the lord for this carrying-service **4½d.** And this carrying-service is worth after receipt 15d. And they will make 4 'berippes' [*sic*], receiving as Thomas Bolter' & Agnes Sprynggold'. And they will prepare for the cart one 'Bedehalfacre', receiving as above, that is to say, 1 loaf; & they will be hayward or reeve & will make common suit; and the value of the carrying-service is 15d. & of the aforesaid 'bederipp'' 12d. and the value of the 'bedehalacre' [*sic*] 3d.; & they will help in making all the hay of the lord appertaining customarily, that is to say, 'North'made', 'Parkemade', 'Shepecotemade' & 'Brodefan'; and the value of such haymaking is 8d.; and they pay yearly	18½d.	18½d.	18½d.	18½d.
John Clerk', Robert Auenant, John Pulley & John Saward' hold one messuage & about 7 acres of land & will do in everything as Thomas Wodward'; & this tenement was formerly Mannes; & they will be hayward & not reeve; value of the carrying service 15d., value of the haymaking 8d., 'bederippes' 12d., 'bedehalfacre' 3d.; and they will pay as yearly rent **3s. 3d.** among themselves, that is to say, from John Clerk' no rent, from R. Auenant **18d.,** from John Polley [*sic*] **14d.,** John Saward' **7d.**	9¾d.	9¾d.	9¾d.	9¾d.
Thomas Hardy holds one messuage & a half virgate of land & will do in all works as Thomas Wodward'; & the value of the carrying service is **15d.,** & the value of 'bederipp'' **12d.,** & the value of the 'Bedeahalacre' [*sic*] **3d.,** & the value of the haymaking 8d., & he will be reeve and hayward & will make common suit &c.	11½d.	11½d.	11½d.	11½d.
John Blunt holds one messuage & 3 quarterlands (*quartronas*) containing 22 and a half acres of land, & will make carrying service in the same way as Thomas Boltere & Agnes &c; and this carrying-service is worth after receipt 2s. 6d. And he will work in autumn as the said Thomas & Agnes & this 'bederippe' is worth 2s. And he will prepare for the cart one 'bedeacr'' as the said Thomas & Agnes; & this 'bedeacr'' is worth 6d. And he will help to mow the aforesaid meadows with 2 men, one with an iron fork; and the value of this haymaking is 16d.; & he will be reeve & hayward	15¾d.	15¾d. 30 eggs	15¾d. 1 ploughshare	15¾d.

John Roger' holds one messuage & 7 acres of land & will do wholly as Thomas Wodward'; & the value of the carrying-service is 15d., & the value of 'bederipp'' 12d., & the value of the 'bedehalfacre' 3d., and the value of the haymaking 8d.; & he will be reeve & hayward & pays	6¼d.	6¼d. 7 eggs	6¼d.	6¼d.
John Bronde holds one messuage & 2 acres of land, & will help to mow all the hay of the lord, which same mowing is worth yearly 8d.; and he will work 4 'bederipp'' which are worth 12d., & one 'bedehalfacre' which is worth yearly 3d.; & he will be reeve or hayward & pays yearly	4¼d. 1 capon	4¼d.	4¼d.	4¼d.
John Stace holds one messuage & 2 acres of land & will do as John Brond'; value of the haymaking 8d., of the 'bederipp'' 12d., of the 'bedehalfacre' 3d.; & he will be as above if &c., & pays yearly, & will make the hedges of the park as J. Richemond', the elder	—	1d.	2 plough-shares	1d.
John Hadstoke holds one messuage & 1 'quarterlond'', & will do as J. Brond'; value of the haymaking **8d.,** value of the 'bederipp'' 12d. and 'bedehalfacre' 3d.; & will be &c.	4½d.	4½d.	4½d.	4½d.
Joan Stace holds one messuage, 2 acres of land sometime 'Flemmynges' & 3 acres of land [*called*] 'Bright'meres' & will help to mow all the meadow of 'North'made' with 1 man, receiving nothing; and this work is worth 2d.; and she will prepare for the cart one 'bederode', receiving half a loaf as the others &c., or will give to the lord 1½d.; & pays rent of 2s. 11d. & pays for one purpresture 1d.	9d.	9d.	9d.	9d.
Monkestrete				
Margaret Crowe[1] holds one messuage & a half virgate of land & 1 acre of land called 'le pightelacre', & will carry with one cart with 2 horses and 2 men hay for a half day, wheat for a half day, oats or pease for a half day, receiving of the lord for this carrying-service 4½d. And this carrying-service is worth after receipt 15d. And she will make 4 'bederippes', receiving as Thomas Bolter' & Agnes Spryngold'. And she will prepare for the cart one 'bedehalf-acre', receiving as above, that is to say, one loaf; and she will be hayward & not reeve & will make common suit & pays yearly	13½d.	13½d.	13½d.	13½d.

[1] 'Hompfrye' added in margin in a later hand.

Boytonende				
John Terry[1] holds one messuage & a half virgate of land & will do in all works as the said Margaret; and the value of the carrying-service 15d., & the value of the 'bederippe' 12d., & the value of the 'bedealfacre'' [*sic*] 4d.; & he will be hayward & pays yearly	12d.	12d.	12d.	12d.
Biewecoteleresgrene				
John Hancok' holds one messuage & 7 acres of land & will do wholly as Thomas Hardy; & the value of the carrying service is 15d., & the value of the 'bederipp'' 12d., & the value of the 'bedehalfacre' 3d., & the value of the haymaking 8d.; & he will be reeve & pays	5d.	5d.	5d.	5d.
Fro Kentesbrugge to Assh'feld'				
John Hyrde, 'smyth'', holds one messuage & 1 'quarterlond'' and will do as John Brond'; value of the haymaking 8d., & of the 'bederipp'' 12d., & of the 'bedehalfacre' 3d.; & he will provide one man for one day to help on the haystacks without receiving anything, & it is worth 2d.; & he will be reeve	6d.	6d.	6d.	6d.
Boytonende				
John Eustace, the younger, holds one messuage & 7 acres of land & will do in everything as J. Brond'; value of the haymaking 8d. & 'bederipp'' 12d., 'bedehalfacre' **3d.**; & he will be reeve and hayward &c.	6d.	6d.	6d.	6d.
Biewecotelesgrene				
John Wale & John Ilger'[2] hold one messuage, 1 'quarterlond'', & will do in everything as J. Brond'; value of the haymaking 8d., value of the 'bederipp'' 12d., & of the 'bedehalfacre' 3d.; & he will be reeve & will help upon the haystacks for a day, value **2d.**	13¼d.	13¼d.	13¼d.	13¼d.
The same John Wale[3] holds in bondage tenure 8 acres of land formerly purchased, & pays yearly	3½d.	3½d.	3½d.	3½d.
John Hardy, 'taillour', holds 6 acres of land in bondage tenure & pays	5¾d.	5¾d.	5¾d.	5¾d.

[1] 'N Hompfrye' added in margin in a later hand.

[2] 'Bul' added in margin in a later hand.

[3] 'Phw' added in margin in a later hand.

Wodhame

Richard Wakelyn holds one messuage & 1 'quarterlond' & will do as John Bronde; value of the haymaking 8d., 'bederepp'' 12d. & 'bedehalfacre' 3d.; & he will be &c., & pays	14d.	14d.	14d.	14d.
The same Richard holds one messuage & one 'quarterlond' & will do as John Bronde; value of the haymaking 8d., of the 'bederipp'' 12d. & 'bedehalfagre' [*sic*] 3d. &c., & pays	6d.	6d.	6d.	6d.
William Fynch' holds one messuage & half an acre of land & will do as John Bronde; value of the haymaking 8d., of the 'bederipp'' 12d. and of the 'bedehalfacre' 3d.; & will be &c.	3d.	3d.	3d.	3d.
John Benge holds 'Mellerslond'' & will do as John Brond'; value of the haymaking 8d., of the 'bederipp'' 12d., 'bedehalfacre' 3d.; & he will be reeve and hayward, & pays &c.	3¼d.	3¼d.	3¼d.	3¼d.
The same John holds one croft & 7 acres of land & will do as John Bronde; value of the haymaking 8d., of the 'bederipp'' 12d., of the 'bedehalfacre' 3d.; & he will be reeve and pays yearly &c.	10d.	10d.	10d.	10d.
The same John holds in demesne and service one toft & 77 acres of land & meadow sometime 'Habrames' & will plough 9 acres at the three seasons or will give to the lord 6s. & will make common suit & pays yearly	22½d.	22½d.	22½d.	22½d.

Biewcotelergrene

William Ilger'[1] holds 6 acres of land & pays yearly	1½d. 2 capons	1½d.	1½d.	1½d.
John Hardy, 'taillour', holds 6 acres of land & pays	—	¾d.	—	1d.
Joan Ilger' holds one messuage & 4 acres of land & will do as John Brond'; value of haymaking 8d., of the 'bederipp'' 12d., of the 'bedehalfacre' 3d.; & she will be &c.	5¼d.	5¼d.	5¼d.	5¼d.
John, son of Walter Hardy, & John Hardy, 'taillour', hold one messuage, 7 acres of land, and will do as John Bronde; value of the haymaking 8d., of the 'bederipp'' 12d., 'bedehalfacr'' 3d.; & they will do suit & will be &c.	6d.	6d.	6d.	6d.

[1] 'Bul' added in margin in a later hand.

Boytonende

John Godard'[1] holds one cottage & 7 acres of land & will do in everything as John Bronde ; value of the 'bedehalueacre' [*blank*], value of the haymaking 8d., value of the 'bederipp'' 12d. ; and he gives 6d. of rent & will be &c.

	1½d.	1½d.	1½d.	1½d.
[*Totals*]	20s.	20s. 1¾d.	20s.	20s. 2¼d.
	4 capons	67 eggs	—	4 plough-shares

Sum 4li. 4½d.

Now of the virgaters & half-virgaters

John Throwere[1] holds one messuage & 1 virgate of land & will make for the lord each year 3 quarters of malt whensoever the lord shall wish or will give to the lord for each quarter **3d.**, & thus 9d. ; & he will plough for winter seed 8 acres, for Lenten seed 8 acres, for fallow 8 acres, or will give to the lord for an acre **4d.** And this ploughing is worth **8s.** And he will work each week 5 works, that is to say, Monday, Tuesday, Wednesday, Thursday & Friday, between the feast of [*Saint*] Michael and the feast of the Nativity of Saint John the Baptist, unless a [*feast*]day occurs, or will give to the lord for each work **½d.** ; and from the feast of the birth of Saint John the Baptist until the feast of Lammas day he will work each week 10 works, unless a feast day shall fall on those days, or will give for each work 1d. ; & from the feast of Lammas day until the feast of [*Saint*] Michael he will work each week 10 works ; during those works he will receive drink (*bibet*), unless a feast day shall befall, or will give to the lord for each work **1d.** And he will mow 9 acres of meadow if it be needed ; he will have an allowance for each acre of two works. And he will have an allowance of 8 works if he work in the meadow for haymaking, not having regard for the number of days on which he will work. And he will make 8 'bederipp'' in Autumn, receiving as the Moolemen, and this work is worth after receipt **4s.** And he will prepare for the cart one 'bedeacre', receiving as the others, & this work is worth 6d. And he will carry as Thomas Boltere & Agnes, receiving as they, for 3 days, & this work is worth after receipt **2s. 6d.** And he will be reeve and hayward if he be chosen & pays no rent, but now he has taken the land aforesaid to farm, paying for all the aforesaid yearly

—	14s.	—	14s.

[1] 'Meade' added in margin in a later hand.

And there is a certain virgate of land called 'Puntes' which was partitioned among all the parceners aforesaid, the lords of this Manor, because it was demised at that time for **30s.** on account of the default of the customary tenant & now it is demised to John Godard' for **20s.**; it used to do in everything as John Throwere & thus the purparty of the lord for 3 parts is now **15s.**	—	7s. 6d.	—	7s. 6d.
John Godard' holds a half virgate of land formerly of Avice Aleyn without a messuage; she used to do the half of all the works as John Throwere & now [*it is held*] to farm & he pays	—	5s. 6d.	—	5s. 6d.
The same John holds one messuage in which he dwells & a half virgate of land, doing the half in everything as John Throwere, but now he pays to farm	—	6s. 8d.	—	6s. 8d.
John Terry holds one messuage & a half virgate of land formerly of Richard Herberde, doing as John Godard', but pays to farm	—	7s.	—	7s.
John Rogier' holds a half virgate of land without a messuage formerly of John Aleyn, doing as John Godarde, but he pays to farm	—	7s.	—	7s.
John Crakeman holds one messuage & a half virgate of land sometime Shymmynges, doing as John Godard'	—	8s.	—	8s.
Walter Trubboc holds one messuage & a half virgate of land formerly Skampes, doing as J.G., & pays yearly	—	9s.	—	9s.
John Thomasongodard' holds one messuage & a half virgate of land formerly of Thomas Godard', doing as above	—	7s.	—	7s.
Richard Wakelyn, Walter Hardy, William Fynch', John Godard, Nicholas Setard' hold one half virgate of land sometime of Hugh Smyth', doing as above, but it is demised to farm & thus they pay	—	6s.	—	6d. [*sic*][1]
Joan Willem holds one messuage & one quarterland (*quartronam*), doing the half of all the works of John Godarde, & gives of rent **3½d.** & for the works **7s.**	—	3s. 7¾d.	—	3s. 7¾d.
John Throwere 'Shether'' holds one messuage & a half virgate of land, doing in everything as John Godard', & pays no rent & gives for the works 14s.	—	7s.	—	7s.
[*Totals*]	—	4li. 8s. 3¾d.	—	4li. 8s. 3¾d.

Sum — 8li. 16s. 7½d.

[1] Should read '6s.'

Now of the Akermen

John Abraham[1] holds one message & 2 'akermanlondes', that is to say, 20 acres of land, and will do every week 4 works between the feast of [*Saint*] Michael and the feast of the Nativity of Saint John the Baptist, and no feast day will not [*sic*] be allowed except for 4 whole weeks, that is to say, for 15 days after the Nativity of the Lord, for the week of Easter and of Pentecost, or he will give or will give [*sic*] to the lord for each work ½d.; & from the feast of the Nativity of Saint John the Baptist until Lammas day, every week, 4 works without allowance of feast days, value of the work **2d.**[2]; & he will help to make [*the hay*] in 4 meadows of the lord until they be mown or will give to the lord for this work 8d., that is to say, with 2 men. And he will make 8 'bederipp'' in Autumn, receiving as the abovesaid customary tenants, & this work is worth after receipt **2s.** And he will prepare for the cart 1 'bedeacr'', receiving 2 loaves as the others, & this work is worth 6d.; & he will help for 2 days on the haystacks without receiving anything of the lord; and he will be reeve & hayward if &c., but now he pays to farm	—	7s.	—	7s.
John Abraham 'Tiler'' holds one message & 10 acres of land & will do the half of all the works of the aforesaid John Abraham & will be reeve & will be hayward and pays &c.	—	3s. 6d.	—	3s. 6d.
John Cartere holds one message & 10 acres of land & will do as John Abraham 'Tilere' in everything, but pays to farm	—	4s.	—	4s.
John Thomassongodarde holds one message & 10 acres of land & will do as the aforesaid John Abraham 'Tyler''	—	3s. 6d.	—	3s. 6d.
John Serle & William Ballarde hold one message & 10 acres of land & will do as J. Abraham	—	4s. 6d.	—	4s. 6d.

Sum — 45s.

Now of the Coterells

John Whateriche holds one toft & 2 acres & one rood of land & will do each week one work between the feast of [*Saint*] Michael & the Nativity of Saint John the Baptist except 4 weeks, for the 15 days [*of the feast*] of the Nativity of the Lord & the weeks of Easter & Pentecost, or will give to the lord for each work **½d.** And from the feast of the Nativity of

[1] 'Meade' added in margin in a later hand.

[2] Should read '1d.'—see pp. 74, 87, 101.

Saint John the Baptist until Lammas-day, every week 1 work, value of the work **1d.** And from Lammas-day until the feast of [*Saint*] Michael, every week 1 work, value of the work **1d.** And he will help to make all the hay of the lord, & this work is worth **8d.** And he will make 4 'bederipp'' as the others &c' or will give to the lord 12d. And he will prepare for the cart one 'bedehalfacre' as &c., or will give to the lord 3d. And he will be reeve & hayward & pays yearly **5d.** of rent & for the works 4s.	—	2s. 2½d.	—	2½d. [*sic*][1]
John Steylwomman holds 1 messuage & 7 acres of land & will do in everything as John Whaterich' & pays of rent yearly **4s.** & for the works **4s.**	—	4s., 1½ eggs	—	4s.
William Hubert holds one messuage, 1 acre 1 rood of land & 1 piece of pasture & will do wholly as John Whaterich' & pays yearly of rent **5d.**, & for the works 3s. 4d.	—	22½d., 1½ eggs	—	22½d.
John Vnderwode holds one messuage & one acre of land & will do as J. Whaterich' & pays no rent but pays	—	2s., 1½ eggs	—	2s.
John Thomasson' Hyrde, the younger, holds one 'coterellond'' without a messuage & will do as J. Whaterich' & pays no rent, but [*pays*] to farm for [*the works*] yearly	—	2s., 1½ eggs	—	2s.
Walter Hardy holds one 'coterellond'' without a messuage, doing as John Whaterich', & gives no rent, but pays for the works to farm.	—	2s., 1½ eggs	—	2s.
[*Totals*]	—	14s. 1d., 7½ eggs	—	14s. 1d.

Total — 28s. 2d.

Now of the Cotmen

Nicholas Setard holds one messuage & one acre of land, anciently arable but now meadow, & will mow until the hay is made & he will receive nothing from the lord & the work is worth 8d. — and he will do 4 'bederipp', receiving as the other customary tenants, & this work is worth 12d.; and he will prepare for the cart one 'bedehalfacre' as above & this work is worth — 3d. And he will make each week between Lammas-day & the feast of [*Saint*] Michael 1 work, value of the work **1d.**, or will give to the lord 8d.; & he will 'dance' [*tripidabit*] on the haystacks for one day or will give to the lord **2d.**; & he gives **12d.** of rent and will be reeve & hayward if &c., & pays to the lord yearly for the works	11¼d.	11¼d.	11¼d.	11¼d.

[1] Should read '2s. 2½d.'

John Vnderwode holds one 'Cotmanlond'' without a messuage & will do in everything as Nicholas Setard' & gives 9d. of rent & for the works 2s. 9d.	10½d.	10½d.	10½d.	10½d.
Walter Hardy holds one messuage & one acre of land & will do in everything as Nicholas Setarde & pays 3s. 1d. of rent & for the works **2s. 9d.**	17½d.	17½d.	17½d.	17½d.
William Wymbussh' holds 3 acres of land without a messuage formerly of Nicholas Hyde, afterwards of Robert Dryby, & will do in everything as Nicholas Setarde & gives **3s.** of rent yearly. And now at farm	—	2s. 6d.	—	2s. 6d.
And[1] be it remembered that all the aforesaid customary tenants who have ploughs by themselves or jointly with the neighbourhood are to come for one day to each 'season' and will plough with the lord for one meal. And that each customary tenant will haulm with the lord for one day for one meal. And that each customary tenant will collect nuts for half a day, receiving nothing of the lord.				
[*Totals*]	4s. 1¾d.	6s. 7¾d.	4s. 1¾d.	6s. 7¾d.

Sum — 21s. 7d.

Feoffees in 'Horham Halle' pay to the lord from the term of 'Hokkeday' by a certain custom called 'Wardepans'	—	—	—	4½d.
Bartholomew Chisehill' gives by the same custom	—	—	—	4¼d.
The Abbot of 'Tilthei' by the same [*custom*]	—	—	—	2d.
William atte Fen by the same	—	—	—	2d.
Henry Boyton' by the same	—	—	—	½d.
John Pannphilon' by the same	—	—	—	½d.
John Richemonde, 'parker', by the same	—	—	—	½d.
John Thrower' the elder by the same custom	—	—	—	1d.
The tenant formerly Puntes by the same custom	—	—	—	1d.
John Godard' by the same	—	—	—	¾d.
The tenant formerly Avis Aleyn by the same	—	—	—	½d.
The tenant formerly Herbert by the same	—	—	—	½d.
The tenants formerly Smythes by the same	—	—	—	½d.
The tenant formerly Shymmynges by the same	—	—	—	½d.
The tenant formerly Aleynnes by the same	—	—	—	½d.

[1] 'Note' added in margin in a later hand.

Joan Willam by the same custom	—	—	—	¼d.
Thomas Boltere & Agnes Spryngold' by the same	—	—	—	1d.
John Blunt by the same	—	—	—	1d.
Thomas Hardy by the same	—	—	—	½d.
Thomas Wodwarde by the same	—	—	—	½d.
John Terry by the same	—	—	—	½d.
Margaret Crowe by the same	—	—	—	½d.
Walter Trubboc by the same	—	—	—	½d.
John Thomasson' Godard' by the same	—	—	—	½d.
Robert Tounsowter' by the same	—	—	—	½d.
John Whaterich' by the same	—	—	—	½d.
Walter Vauasour by the same	—	—	—	½d.
John Colman by the same custom	—	—	—	½d.
The tenant of Walter Crowe by the same custom	—	—	—	½d.
William Gile by the same	—	—	—	½d.
John Taillour by the same custom	—	—	—	¼d.
John Peserissh', John Rogier' (¼d.), John Eustas, the younger (¼d.), John Brond' (¼d.), by the same custom	—	—	—	1d.
John Stelewomman by the same	—	—	—	¼d.
	2s. 5¼d.			

Sum of the rents of the freemen yearly	10li. 2s. 11¾d.	
Sum of capons 13		
Sum of the value of the same	4s. 4d.	
Sum of hens 2		
Sum of the value of the same	4d.	
Sum of ploughshares 2		
Sum of the value of the same	2s.	
Sum of geese 4		
Sum of the value of the same	16d.	
Sum of cumin 1 lb.		
Sum of the value of the same	3d.	
Sum of the rents of the Moolmen	4li. 4½d.	
Sum of the value of their works	71s. ½d.	
Sum of capons 4		
Sum of the value of the same	16d.	
Sum of eggs 67		
Sum of the value of the same	3½d.	
Sum of ploughshares 4		
Sum of the value of the same	4s.	
Sum of the farms of the bond-tenants for their works, that is to say, as well for rent as for all the abovenamed from virgaters, half-virgaters, akermen, coterells & cotmen	13li. 11s. 4½d.	
Sum of eggs 7½		
Sum of the value of the same	¼d.	
Sum of 'wardesiluer''	2s. 5¼d.	

Further for the value of 2 carrying services of hay & corn

And note that as it was said that the tenants have among themselves a custumal other than that destroyed at the time of the rebellion & do not wish to tell the lord's council at present, therefore by the custom of the council now present the custom is that they pay for their works as is above specified, & therefore &c.

Sum of all these sums — (31li. 19s. 7d. *struck through*, 32li. 2s. 7¼d. *interlined*).

Now of the Burgage-tenants

Parkestrete

John Wolpit holds one messuage & owes 2 attendances at the court, at 1 leet & 1 court, held after the feast of [*Saint*] Michael & Easter, or will be bailiff of the borough if chosen &c., & pays	—	6d.	—	6d.
The same holds one purpresture & pays	—	½d.	—	½d.
John Sparowe holds one messuage & pays	—	6d.	—	6d.
John Rennere holds one messuage & pays	—	1½d.	—	1½d.
The same holds 31 perches of 'Countesgardyn' & pays	—	15¾d.	—	15¾d.
John Coppyng' holds one messuage & pays	—	3d.	—	3d.
The same holds 13¼ perches there & pays	—	6½d.	—	6½d.
Adam Hamond' & John Herlyng' hold one messuage	—	4½d.	—	4½d.
The same Adam holds 15½ perches there in the same way & pays	—	7¾d.	—	7¾d.
The same John Herlyng' holds 5¼ perches & pays	—	2½d.	—	2¾d.
John Smyth' & William Spyng' hold one messuage & pay	—	3d.	—	3d.
The same John & William Spyng' hold 21½ perches in the aforesaid way & pay	—	10¾d.	—	10¾d.
Walter Coraunt holds 11½ perches in the like way & pays	—	5¾d.	—	5¾d.
Roger Gamelyn holds 29½ perches in the like way & pays	—	14¾d.	—	14¾d.
Thomas Warrewyk' holds one messuage & pays	—	4¼d.	—	4¼d.
The same Thomas holds 15¾ perches in the same way & pays	—	7¾d.	—	8d.
John Bradfeld' & John Herry hold 2 messuages & pay	—	15¾d.	—	15¾d.
The same John Bradfeld' holds 19¼ perches in the aforesaid way	—	9½d.	—	9¾d.
The same John Herry holds 27 perches in the aforesaid garden	—	13½d.	—	13½d.
William Asshele holds one purpresture & pays	—	¼d.	—	¼d.
John Kent & Thomas Ware hold 1 purpresture	—	1d.	—	1d.
John Kent holds one purpresture next 'Chaloneresbrigge'	—	¼d.	—	¼d.
Thomas Ware holds one messuage & pays	—	1½d.	—	1½d.
John Herlyng' holds one messuage & pays	—	½d.	—	½d.
John Sparrowe holds one messuage & pays	—	4d.	—	4d.

The same John holds one messuage & pays	—	3½d.	—	3½d.
The same John holds one messuage & pays	—	10½d.	—	10½d.
Thomas Boltere holds one messuage & pays	—	1d.	—	1d.
John Cornewaile holds one messuage & pays	—	1d.	—	1d.
John Shethere holds 2 messuages & pays	—	11¾d.	—	11¾d.
John Lighfot holds one messuage & pays	—	2d.	—	2d.
John Herry, 'brewer', holds one messuage & pays	—	2s. 9d.	—	2s. 9d.
Robert Gile holds one messuage & pays	—	5¼d.	—	5¼d.
John Venour holds [*one*] messuage & pays	—	3d.	—	3d.
William Shethere holds one messuage & pays	—	8d.	—	8d.
The same William holds one purpresture & pays	—	6d.	—	6d.
Thomas Barbour holds one messuage & pays	—	2d.	—	2d.
William Pamphilon' holds one parcel of the lord's garden & pays	—	9d.	—	9d.
John Spilman holds one messuage & pays	—	6½d.	—	6¾d.
The same holds one postern-gate towards 'Berneyerde', leading from his messuage	—	½d.	—	½d.
The same holds one piece of land next 'le Bernegate', containing in length 24 feet and in breadth 16 feet; he will make a house with a room, under which room he will make a gate suitable for entrance to the grange and curtilage, for opening & shutting at the order of those entering, whensoever they shall wish; which same gate he shall maintain at his own costs & pays	—	3d.	—	3d.
William Patergos holds one messuage & pays	—	6½d.	—	6¾d.
Richard Boxeued, the younger, holds one messuage & pays	—	6½d.	—	6½d.
The same holds one purpresture & pays	—	1d.	—	1d.
Thomas Boltere holds one shop & pays	—	2¼d.	—	2¼d.
Thomas Sherman holds one shop	—	2¼d.	—	2¼d.
William Gile holds one shop & pays	—	2¼d.	—	2¼d.
Thomas Petit & his associates, feoffees of J. Michell', hold one vacant piece of ground	—	2d.	—	2d.
John Spilman holds one messuage purchased of Walter Reymont & pays	—	2¼d.	—	2¼d.
The same holds 3 purprestures there & pays	—	2½d.	—	2½d.

John Clerc & Richard Gile hold 1 butcher's-shop	—	2¼d.	—	2¼d.
William Spilman holds one house & pays yearly	—	2½d.	—	2½d.

Fro ye Hallegate to ye chirch'stile

Thomas Yerdele holds one messuage & pays yearly	—	11½d.	—	11½d.
The churchwardens hold one piece of ground purchased of Thomas Yerdelee where the church stile is, & pay yearly	—	2d.	—	2d.
Thomas Yerdelee holds 1 purpresture at the church stile & pays yearly	—	½d.	—	½d.

Fro kyrestile to ye Westende of ye chirchyerd'

Walter atte Lane holds one garden & pays	—	2½d.	—	2½d.
Thomas Yerdele holds one piece of the lord's garden in 'le Courteyerde', containing in length 12 feet & in width 32 feet, paying yearly **18d.** Nothing here because among the rents & new farms of the 16th. year at the end, as appears in a certain rental thereof made		nothing		
William Gay holds one garden & pays	—	1½d.	—	1½d.
The same William holds one purpresture & pays yearly **16d.** Nothing for the reason aforesaid		nothing		
The same William holds one piece of the lord's garden & pays yearly **12d.** Nothing for the reason aforesaid		nothing		
Thomas Grendale holds one messuage & pays yearly	—	3½d.	—	3½d.
Thomas Grendale holds one piece of the lord's garden & pays	—	5d.	—	5d.

Bulfordestrete

Joan Colle holds one shop & pays yearly	—	1¼d.	—	1¼d.
John Fox holds one shop & pays yearly	—	1¼d.	—	1¼d.
John Brigge holds one shop & pays yearly	—	1¼d.	—	1¼d.
Thomas Vfford', the vicar, holds one messuage	—	6½d.	—	6½d.
John Terry holds one messuage & pays yearly **2½d.** And holds one curtilage & pays **3d.**	—	2¾d.	—	2¾d.
The same John holds one purpresture & pays yearly	—	8d.	—	8d.
Thomas Warewyk' holds one messuage & pays	—	4½d.	—	4½d.
Richard Bateman holds one messuage & pays	—	1½d.	—	1½d.
The same holds one purpresture in 'bolefordgardyne' recently enclosed & pays yearly	—	12d.	—	12d

Thomas Warrewyk' holds one messuage & pays	—	1½d.	—	1½d.
The same Thomas holds one purpresture in 'bolefordegardy' [*sic*] & pays yearly	nothing at present, because he does not agree with the steward about the same			
Walter Essex holds one messuage & pays	—	2d.	—	2d.
The same Walter holds one purpresture in 'Bolefordgardyn'	nothing here at present for the reason aforesaid			
Thomas Wymbussh' holds one purpresture there	nothing here for the reason aforesaid			
John Jeray holds one messuage there : nothing	nothing for the reason expressed			
Richard Hamond' holds one purpresture	nothing for the reason aforesaid			
John atte Water' holds one messuage & pays	—	6d.	—	6d.
Andrew Neel holds one messuage & pays	—	3d.	—	3d.
John Venour holds one messuage & pays	—	6d.	—	6d.
John Ewayn holds one messuage & pays	—	3d.	—	3d.
John Richemond, 'Pulter', holds one messuage & pays	—	3d.	—	3d.
The same holds one purpresture in 'bolefordegardyn' & pays	nothing for the reason aforesaid			
William Hale holds one garden & pays	—	3d.	—	3d.
John Jeray holds one messuage & pays	—	3d.	—	3d.
The same holds one purpresture in 'bolefordgardyn' & pays				
William Botelmaker' holds one purpresture there				
John Lonered' holds one purpresture there & pays	nothing at present for the reason aforesaid			
Thomas Venour holds one purpresture there				
John Venour, the younger, holds one purpresture there & pays				
William Botelmaker' holds one messuage & pays	—	2d.	—	2d.
John Lonerede holds one messuage & pays	—	2d.	—	2d.
Andrew Neel holds one purpresture & pays	—	2d.	—	2d.
Thomas Sherman holds [*one*] purpresture	—	1½d.	—	1½d.

Between the cemetery and the highway

John Dod' holds one shop & pays	—	½d.	—	½d.
John Copcy holds one shop	—	—	—	½d.

Fro Margaretewell' to Shepecotelane

Roger atte Felde holds one purpresture before his messuage	—	½d.	—	½d.
The same Roger & John Stile, the younger, hold 2 messuages	—	2d.	—	2d.
Thomas Warewyk' holds one messuage & pays	—	4½d.	—	4½d.
Thomas Venour holds one purpresture & pays	—	¼d.	—	¼d.
John Treweman holds one purpresture & pays	—	¼d.	—	¼d.
Roger Hikedy holds one messuage & pays	—	5¼d.	—	5¼d.
Robert Fader' holds one messuage & pays	—	1d.	—	1d.
Richard Skilman holds one messuage & pays	—	11½d.	—	11½d.
The same holds one postern & pays yearly	—	—	—	¼d.
The same holds one purpresture & pays	—	1½d.	—	1½d.
Thomas Maij holds one messuage & pays	—	9¾d.	—	9¾d.
The same holds one purpresture & pays	—	1d.	—	1d.
John Boyton' holds one purpresture in 'Newefelde'	—	1½d.	—	1½d.
Joan Haftere holds one messuage & pays	—	5¾d.	—	5¾d.
John Shethere holds one messuage & pays	—	6½d.	—	6½d.
Thomas Mannyng' holds one messuage & pays	—	8¾d.	—	8¾d.
The same holds 2 purprestures & pays	—	2d.	—	2d.
John Camberleyn holds one messuage & pays	—	4d.	—	4d.
Thomas Boltere holds one messuage & pays	—	13d.	—	13d.
The same Thomas holds 3 purprestures & pays yearly	—	2½d.	—	2½d.
Walter Clerk' holds one messuage	—	5¼d.	—	5¼d.
The same Walter holds one postern & pays yearly	—	½d.	—	½d.
William Wymbussh' holds one messuage & pays yearly	—	5¼d.	—	5¼d.
John Boyton holds a half rood in 'Newefeld' & pays	—	1½d.	—	1½d.

Shepecotelane

John Kent holds one messuage next Kentesbridge & pays	—	2d.	—	2d.
The same John holds one purpresture there where the hall is built	—	1d.	—	1d.

Fro Kentesbridge to Asshfeldfotewey

John Kent holds one messuage & pays yearly	—	9¾d.	—	9¾d.
The same holds one purpresture & pays yearly	—	3d.	—	3d.
Andrew Droght holds one messuage & pays yearly	—	2d.	—	2d.
Walter Walkelyn holds one messuage & pays	—	2d.	—	2d.
The same Walter holds one purpresture & pays	—	2d.	—	2d.
John Essex holds one messuage & pays	—	1d.	—	1d.
The same holds one purpresture & pays	—	1d.	—	1d.
William Shethere holds one messuage & pays yearly	—	1d.	—	1d.
John Auenant holds one garden & pays	—	½d.	—	½d.
Alianora Wolpit holds one messuage & pays	—	2d.	—	2d.
John Baron' holds one messuage & pays yearly	—	1d.	—	1d.
Thomas Goldebeter' holds one messuage & pays	—	1d.	—	1d.
The same holds one purpresture & pays	—	1d.	—	1d.

Fro litelbrigge to Millehach'

John Kent holds one messuage & pays	—	3d.	—	3d.
Ralph Essex' holds one messuage	—	3½d.	—	3½d.

ye Midelrowe

William Patergos holds one vacant piece of ground at the head of 'Midelrowe' & pays yearly	—	3d.	—	3d.
Matilda Wakeleyn holds one messuage & pays yearly	—	1½d.	—	1½d.
Nicholas Herlyng' holds one messuage	—	4d.	—	4d.
Richard Broxeuede holds one messuage & pays yearly	—	1½d.	—	1½d.
Alice Hayward' holds one messuage & pays yearly	—	2½d.	—	2½d.
Walter Clerc holds one messuage & pays	—	3d.	—	3d.
The same Walter holds one purpresture & pays yearly	—	½d.	—	½d.
Walter Russhedale holds 2 messuages & pays yearly	—	5d.	—	5d.
The same Walter holds 1 purpresture & pays	—	½d.	—	½d.
John Raufson', 'shethere', holds one messuage	—	1d.	—	1d.
Andrew Sibbe holds one messuage & pays yearly	—	2d.	—	2d.
The same holds one purpresture & pays yearly	—	½d.	—	½d.
John atte Style holds one shop & pays	—	½d.	—	½d.
John Venour holds 2 shops & pays yearly	—	1d.	—	1d.

Fro chirchestile to cornerhoppes [*sic*] *on either side*

Thomas Yerdele holds one shop under the solar next the smithy of R. Saucer' & pays yearly	—	1½d.	—	1½d.
John Boyton' holds one shop & pays yearly	—	2d.	—	2d.
William Symond' holds one shop & pays yearly	—	2d.	—	2d.
Elena Loksmyth' holds one shop & pays yearly	—	2d.	—	2d.
John Elmeswell' holds one shop and pays yearly	—	2d.	—	2d.
John Legat holds one messuage & pays yearly	—	10¾d.	—	10¾d.
Walter Boyton' holds one messuage & pays	—	2¾d.	—	2¾d.
William Gay holds one messuage & pays yearly	—	2½d.	—	2½d.
Gilbert Goldebeter' holds one messuage & pays	—	3½d.	—	3½d.
John Smyth', 'codewaner'', holds one messuage	—	3d.	—	3d.
The same John holds one purpresture & pays	—	½d.	—	½d.
John Judde holds one messuage & pays yearly	—	2d.	—	2d.
The same John holds one purpresture & pays yearly	—	½d.	—	½d.
John Abraham, 'tyler'', holds 'Nethercornershoppe' on the south part & pays yearly	—	3¼d.	—	3¼d.
The same holds there 2 purprestures & pays yearly	—	2¼d.	—	2¼d.
J[ohn] Richemond', the elder, holds one messuage & pays	—	4d.	—	4d.
John Courthose holds one shop & pays	—	1½d.	—	1½d.
Richard Boxeued' holds one messuage & pays	—	3d.	—	3d.
Robert Auenant holds one messuage & pays	—	13½d.	—	13½d.
The same Robert holds one purpresture & pays	—	1d.	—	1d.

be nethe nethre north' chirch'stile

Thomas Bisshop' holds one shop & pays	—	¾d.	—	¾d.
Robert Fader' holds one shop & pays	—	¾d.	—	¾d.
Walter atte Lane holds one messuage	—	1½d.	—	1½d.
Walter Bakere holds one shop	—	½d.	—	½d.
From the farm of the stalls in the market-place	—	19½d.	—	19½d.
From the tolls of the market & fairs	—	22½d.	—	22½d.
[*Totals*]	—	54s. 1d.	—	54s. 2¼d.

Sum — 108s. 3¼d.

Now of the farmer-tenants of lands falling into the hands of the lord by escheat and for default of tenants, &c.

Nicholas Richemond holds 3 parts of 'Duketeslond''	—	9s.	—	9s.
Henry Munde holds 3 parts of 'Pamphiloneslond''	—	4s. 6d.	—	4s. 6d.
Thomas Thrower'[1] holds one croft of arable land with one curtilage formerly of Rullico	—	13d.	—	13d.
John Bienge holds 5 roods of meadow in 'North'mede'	—	2s.	—	2s.
John Aleyn holds 'Bailliescroft' next 'Boxstede'	—	13d.	—	13d.
William Clerevaux holds one toft formerly of Richard Daweber' & pays yearly	—	12d.	—	12d.
[*Totals*]	—	18s. 8d.	—	18s. 8d.

Sum — 37s. 4d.

Sum of the total up to here — 39li. 5s. 2¼d.

Be it remembered that all the aforesaid rents have been debited in the next compotus, except particulars newly taken in 'Countesgardyn' as appears in 'Parkestrete'. And that no new rent of this year is debited in this rental, except 12d. from Coke, 'Shether'', & 6d. from J. Spilman. And that no mention is made of demesne lands [*and*] meadows, because without the steward & the rolls of the preceding compoti it is not possible to do so at present, & especially until the court-rolls are made in full.

Now of the demesne & firstly of the Site of the Manor, 17 acres 3 roods 1 perch.

John Herry, 'bocher'', holds to farm the gardens of the lord aforesaid for a term of 12 years in addition to a certain portion still being farmed out to him of 'Bulfordstete' [*sic*] & pays. And the aforesaid John will maintain & look after all the enclosure of the said gardens during his term.	—	28s. 4d.	—	28s. 4d.

[End of roll. See Introduction, p. 1]

[1] 'Meade' added in margin in a later hand.

BAILIFF'S ACCOUNT, 1361-62

Thaxsted'

Account of Simon Crowe, Bailiff of Lady Isabell, daughter of the King of England, in his Manor there [from the feast][1] of Saint Michael the Archangel, in the 35th year of the reign of King Edward the third after the Conquest, until the Morrow of Saint Michael next following [in the 36th year of the aforesaid King, that is to say, for one][1] whole [year].[1]

[*Arrears*][1]

19li. 2s. 2½d. Sum 19li. 2s. 2½d.

Rents of Assize [*& external rents*][1]

The same answers for 4li. 5s. 2½d. from the rents of assize at the term of the Nativity of the Lord. And for 105s. 8½d. received from the rents of assize at Easter. And for 4li. 2s. 11¾d. from the rents of assize at the term of the Nativity of Saint John the Baptist. And for 107s. 4¾d. from the rents of assize at the term of Saint Michael. And for 3s. 1¾d. received from 'Wardpans' at 'Hokeday' yearly. And for 2d. received from 1 pound of cumin from the rents at the term of Easter sold as without. [Unfixed rent *added in margin in a different hand.*] And for 10½d. received from 7 arrows from the rents at the term of Easter sold as without. And for 8s. from 8 ploughshares sold from the rents of the term of Saint Botolph. And for 1d. from the new rent [of][1] William Tile at the term of Saint Michael. And for 1d. from the new rent of John Blake for 1 piece of ground taken from the highway, at the 4 terms [now of Edmund Venour contained in Rental *interlined in a different hand*]. [And for][1] ¼d. from the increase of the rent of William Saucer [not contained in Rental *interlined in a different hand*] for 1 piece of bond meadow purchased from Nicholas atte Hyde in 'Lorimers-croft', at the term of Saint [Michael. And][1] for ¼d. received from William Drought for half an acre of meadow purchased from John Saucer' [not contained in Rental *interlined in a different hand*]. And for ½d. at the terms of Easter [& Saint Michael][1] received from the increase of the rent of Walter atte Fen for 1 piece of bond meadow purchased from William Botild'. And for ½d. from the new rent of [Walter][1] Habraham at the term of Saint Michael for 1 piece taken from the highway at 'Richemondesgrene' [contained in Rental *interlined in a different hand*]. And for ½d. from the increase of the rent of John Clerk' for 1 piece of pasture lying in 'Wynterwellemad'', at the terms of Easter and Saint Michael [contained in Rental *interlined in a different hand*]. And for 2d. at the same terms received from the new rent of John Bienge for a certain purpresture demised to him in the high road towards 'Dunmowe', at the head of 'Middelrowe', next the messuage of the said John [of the charge of the reeve of the borough *interlined in a different hand*]. And for ½d. from the increase of the rent of William Baker' for 1 rood of meadow & 1 acre of land which he purchased of Joan Peyt, bondwoman of the lord,[2] at the terms of Easter & Saint Michael. [Bakere not contained in Rental *interlined in a different hand*].

Sum 19li. [16s. 3¼d. *struck through,* 14s. (9 *struck through*) ¼d. *interlined in a different hand*].

Sum [15li. *struck through,* 19li. 14s. ¼d. *interlined, all in a different hand*].

Rents [*of assize of the borough & tolls*][1] *of the market & fairs*

The same answers for 46s. 7½d. received from the rents of the borough at the term of Easter. And for 46s. 7½d. received from the rents of Saint [Michael][1]. And for 4s. 4d. received from the farm of the stalls in the market place at the terms of Easter and Saint Michael. And for 5s. received from the tolls of the market [at the same][1] terms. And for 6d. received from the new rent of Thomas Lihtfot for 1 piece of land at the eastern head of the grange of the manor. [And for][1] 16d. from the new rent of Walter atte Hyde for 1 piece of land from the lord's garden next his messuage. And

[1] Illegible, word(s) supplied.

[2] The scribe frequently forgets that Isabel, daughter of Edward III, had possession of the manor.

for 4d. from the new rent of Walter Walklyn opposite his tenement [*sic*], at the same terms. And for 1d. from the new rent of Walter Camberleyn, for 1 purpresture next his house. And for 2d. from the new rent of John Frend' for 1 piece of ground in the enclosure of the manor between the granary of the lord and his house, at the same terms. And for ½d. from the new rent of John Delauill' for 1 piece of land in 'Bolefordegardyn', at the same terms. And for 4d. from the new rent of William Coteler' for 1 piece of land within the manor next the granary on the eastern part. And for 4d. from the new rent of Robert de Cretyngg' for 1 piece of land there at the same terms. And for ¼d. from the new rent of John Latonner' for a certain footway next his garden through a postern-gate as far as 'Newefeld'', at the term of Saint Michael yearly. And for 1d. from the new rent of John Frend' for 1 piece of a curtilage between the granary & the room of the steward, containing 40 feet in length & 8 feet in breadth, at the terms of Easter and Saint Michael. And for 1½d. from the new rent of William Lyonn for 2 purprestures in the market-place next the eastern stile of the churchyard, thus demised to him, at the same terms. And for 1d. from the new rent of Walter Camberleyn for 1 piece of land next his house at the same terms. And for 4d. from William atte Grene for 2 purprestures demised to the same at the will of the lord in burgage, next his house, as they are divided by the metes and bounds, at the terms aforesaid. And for 6d. received from Walter Alwyne for 1 piece between his messuage & the great ditch leading from 'Asshfeld'' towards the bridge, in burgage of the town aforesaid, as it is divided by the metes, thus demised to the same, at the terms aforesaid. And for 4s. received from Thomas Lihtfot for 1 parcel of the lord's garden below his messuage thus demised to the same, at the terms aforesaid. And for 6d. from Robert Cretyngg' for one vacant piece of land on the south part of his house thus demised at the will of the lady, at the same terms. And for 1d. from Richard Wolmar' for 1 piece of land of the soil of the manor from the high street of 'Thaxsted'' thus demised at the will of the lord, at the terms aforesaid. And for ½d. from Roger atte Welde for 1 piece taken from the high street, to hold at the will of the lord, at the terms aforesaid. And for 1d. from William Loksmyth' for 1 piece of land of the soil of the manor from the high street, at the will of the lord, at the terms aforesaid.

Sum 5li. 11s. 6¾d.

Issue of both demesne lands and lands in the hands of the lord by death

He answers for 20s. received from the farm of 1 virgate of land, sometime of John Punt & Hugh Punt, yearly, thus demised to [John *interlined*] Thrower [now of John Godard *interlined in a different hand*], at the 4 principal terms. And for 18s. received from the farm of 40 acres of land, sometime 'Duketteslond', demised to John Wychebaud', now in the hand of John Bienge to farm at the will of the lord, at the same terms. And for 12s. received from the farm of 16 acres of land & 1 acre of meadow, sometime of Pamfylonn, demised to John Danyel, at the same terms. And for 6s. 8d. received from the farm of 20 acres of demesne land in 'Northfeld'' demised to John Bienge, at the same terms. And for 5s. received from Robert Dryby [now the vicar *interlined in a different hand*] for the farm of 1 croft, sometime of Nicholas atte Hyde, yearly, thus demised to the same for his whole life. [For 1 croft, sometime of Nicholas atte Hyde, demised for **2s.** Now John Henry holds *added in margin in a different hand*]. And for 2s. [2s. 2d. *interlined*] from the new farm of Thomas de Woubourn' for 1 croft of land with 1 piece of curtilage called 'Rollecorscroft', thus demised to the same for the term of his life, at the same terms. And for 7s. 6d. received from John Clerk' from the farm of 13 acres 3 roods of demesne land in 'Boxsted'' with 1 piece of pasture called 'Alsichewell'', thus demised to the same, at the same terms. And for 2s. 8d. received from the farm of 5 acres of demesne land there demised to Margery Essex', at the same terms, at the will of the lord. And for [5s. *struck through,* 4s. *interlined*] from the farm of 5 roods of meadow in 'Northmad'' demised to John Bienge, at the same terms. And for 7s. from the farm of ½ virgate of land, sometime of Herberd', thus demised to John Thrower', at the same terms. And for 16s. 6d. from the farm of ½ virgate of land, sometime of Shymmyng', thus demised to William Hadestok', at the same terms. And for 5s. 6d. from the farm of a tenement of 1 akerman, that is to say, of John Peyt, thus demised to John Habraham, at the same terms. And for 5s. 6d. from the farm of a tenement of 1 akerman [*illegible*] of

John Cok', thus demised to the same John Habraham, at the same terms. And for 2s. 6d. from the farm of 'Bretonneslond'', of coterell tenure, demised to Alan Shepherde, at the same terms. And for 20d. from the farm of 1 croft of land, sometime of John Ballie, lying next the mill of 'Cherchemell'', thus demised to John Lok', at the same terms, while the lord shall please. And for 3s. received from the farm of 6 acres of land, formerly land, formerly in the hand of William Fromund, thus demised to William Hadestok' & Joan his wife & to William, the son of the same, at the will of the lady, at the same terms. And for 2s. from the farm of 1 piece of land containing 2 acres in 'le Worthen', thus demised to John Hunt at the will of the lord, at the same terms. And for 11s. [10s. *interlined in a different hand*] from the farm of a half virgate of land, sometime of Amice Alein, thus demised to John Godard', at the same terms. And for 12s. [10s. *interlined in a different hand*] from the farm of a half virgate of land, sometime of William Mascal, thus demised to William Chopyn this year.

Sum 7li. 5s. 6d.

New Farms

He answers for 24li. 3s. 9d. received from demesne lands, meadows and pastures demised to divers men this year, as appears by 1 bill of the parcels annexed to this roll.

Sum 24li. 3s. 9d.

Issue of the Manor

He answers for 9¾d. received from 195 eggs sold for **20 a 1d.** For pasture along the headlands in 'Boxsted'', in 'Newefeld'', in 'le Worthen', in 'Northfeld'' & in 'Asshfeld'', nothing rendered here because it is demised as a whole among lands & pastures of the demesne, as appears by 1 bill of the same, as above.

Sale of hay

And for 14s. 4d. received from Walter Walklyn for 3 haycocks in 'Parkmad'' thus sold to him. And for 5s. received from John Henry for 1 haycock there thus sold to him. And for 13s. 4d. received from William Wolpet for 3 haycocks there thus sold to him. And for 14s. received of William Loksmyth' for 3 haycocks there thus sold to him. And for 100s. received of Robert Arneburgh', purveyor (*prouisore*) of lord Walter de Mauny, for 20 haycocks there thus sold to him.

Sale of wood

And for 30s. 10d. received from divers men for appletrees and peartrees in the garden thrown down by the wind sold to the same, whose names and parcels appear by 1 bill. And for 109s. 4d. received from divers men for 4100 faggots in the park of 'Southfrith'' thus sold this year, that is to say, for 100 faggots **2s. 8d.**, whose names and parcels appear by 1 bill. And for 22s. received of 1100 faggtos sold in the little park, for 100 faggots **2s.** And for 13s. 4d. received from Thomas Subourn' for 500 faggots in the park of 'Southfrith'' thus sold to him, for 100 faggots **2s. 8d.** And for 6s. 8d. received from John Hadestoke for 1 acre of underwood in the park called 'Southfrith'' sold to him. And for 20d. from 1 rood of underwood there sold to John Spryngold'. And for 22s. 6d. received from divers men for 4½ acres of underwood in the little park thus sold at the value per **acre 5s.**, whose names & parcels appear by bill.

Sum 17li. 13s. 9¾d.

Agistment of the parks

He answers for 19s. 10d. received from divers beasts agisted in the park of 'Southfrith'' this year, except tithes, & beyond the beasts agisted for the fee of the parker. And for 18s. 5½d. received from divers beasts agisted in the little park, except tithes, this year, as appears by 1 bill of the names and parcels.

Sum 38s. 3½d.

Works & customs sold

He answers for 3s. 6¾d. received from the making of 14 quarters 2 bushels of malt sold at the value per quarter **3d.** And for 38s. received from 114 acres of ploughing sold to customary tenants at the value of each acre **4d.** And for 38s. 7¾d. from 927¾ winter works at the value per work **½d.** And for 11s. 6d. received from 138 summer works sold at the value per work **1d.** And for 49s. 0½d. received from 588½ autumn works sold at the value per work **1d.**

Sum 7li. [13s. *struck through*] 11d.

Sale of corn

He answers for 57s. 2d. received from 10 quarters 5 bushels 3 pecks of wheat received from the farm of the mills this year at the value per quarter **5s. 4d.** And for 50s. 0¼d. — received from 10 quarters 5 bushels 3 pecks of the multure of the said mills at the value per quarter **4s. 8d.**

Sum 5li. 7s. 2¼d.

Stock sold

He answers for 12d. received from 4 geese of rent sold at the value per head 3d. And for 7s. 6d. received from 30 capons of rent sold at the value per head **3d.** And for 4d. received from 2 hens of rent sold.

Sum 8s. 10d.

Perquisites of the Courts & Leet

He answers for 4li. 11s. 2d. received from the Court held Monday next after the feast of St. Dyonisius. And for 14s. 5d. from the Court held Monday next before the feast of St. Martin the Bishop. And for 13s. 3d. from the Court held Tuesday next after the feast of St. Nicholas the Bishop. And for 10s. from the Court held Friday in the week of the Nativity of the Lord. And for 9s. 10d. from the Court held Thursday next before the feast of the Purification of the Blessed Mary. And for 22s. received from the Court held Thursday next after the feast of St. Juliana. And for 12s. from the Court held Thursday next after the feast of the Annunciation of the Blessed Virgin Mary. And for 8s. 4d. from the Court held Monday next after the feast of Saints Philip & James. And for 44s. 11d. from the Leet held the same day. And for 9s. 11d. from the Court held Monday next after the feast of the Ascension of the Lord. And for 16s. 3d. from the Court held Tuesday next after the feast of St. James the Apostle.

Sum 12li. 12s. 1d.

Sum total of receipts with arrears 120li. 18s. 4d.

Allowances and deductions of rents

In deduction of the rent of a tenement, sometime Panphylonns, because in the hand of the lord & at farm as above, at the 4 terms abovesaid, 4s. 4d. In deduction of the rent of 1 croft, sometime of Nicholas atte Hyde, for the aforesaid reason, 3s. In deduction of the rent of 1 piece of ground, sometime of William Dauy & Robert Carpenter', being in the hand of the lord, and the ditch (*fouea*) is made for enclosing the lord's garden from 'Bolefordegardin' unto the piece of ground, sometime of Pykel, at the terms of Easter & St. Michael, 16½d. In deduction of the rent of 1 piece of ground, sometime of Geoffrey Ilger', Robert Cappe & Philip Smith (*Faber*), because in the hand of the lord & lying vacant, at the same terms, 10d. In deduction of the rent of 1 piece of ground of Osebert Anable & Geoffrey Miller (*Molend'*), lying in the highway unto 'Berdefeld'', because in the hand of the lady & vacant, at the same terms, 6d. In deduction of the rent of the stallage, sometime of Thomas Monioye, because in the hand of the lord & lies vacant, at the same terms, 2d. In deduction of the rent of 1 croft of land containing 1½ acres, sometime of John Ballie, because in the hand of the lord & at farm above, at the 4 terms aforesaid, 2s. 2d. In deduction of the rent of 1 stallage, sometime of Andrew Compagnon, because in the hand of the lord & stands vacant, 2d. In deduction of the rent of 1 stallage, sometime of William atte Noke & William Homan, for the aforesaid reason, 2d. In deduction of the rent of 1 stallage, sometime of Henry Hendrys, for the aforesaid reason, 2d. In deduction of the rent of 1 stallage, sometime of Adam de Seint Albons & Nicholas atte Hyde, for the aforesaid reason, 2d. In deduction of 1 stallage, sometime of Richard Horel, for the aforesaid reason, 2d. In deduction of the rent of 1 stallage, sometime of William atte Hel, for the aforesaid reason, 2d. In deduction of the rent of 1 stallage, sometime of Jane de Berdefeld' and William Tanner', for the aforesaid reason, 2d. In deduction of the rent of 3 stallages, sometime of John Pullekoo, for the aforesaid reason, 6d. In deduction of the rent of 1 stallage, sometime of Edmund Danyel, for the aforesaid reason, 2d. In deduction of the rent of 1 stallage, sometime of Richard Arnald' & Roger Hoberd', for the aforesaid reason, 2d. In deduction of the rent of 1 stallage, sometime of John Pountfreyt, for the aforesaid reason, 2d. In deduction of the rent of 1 stallage, sometime of John Hydeman & William son of John Shather', for the aforesaid reason, 2d. In deduction of the rent of 1 stallage, sometime of John Spayne & Thomas Fatbaconn, for the aforesaid reason, 2d.

14s. 10½d.

Necessaries

In 6340 faggots made as without — 42s. 2½d., for **100, 8d.** In parchment bought as well for the rolls and examinations of the Court, as for the final account thence made yearly, 2s. In payment of John Neel hired for 24 days to mend the fence around 'Bolefordegardyn' because thrown down by the blast of wind 8s., taking per day **4d.** In payment of 1 lad (*garc'*) hired for the same during the same time, 4s., taking per day **2d.** In payment of John Pirie hired for 6 days to enclose anew 'le Pountfolde' with palings 18d., taking per day **3d.**

Sum 57s. 8½d.

Cost of the houses and mills

In payment of John Neel hired for 5 days to right and repair the cowshed & 'le Garyte' almost thrown down by the exceptional blowing of the wind 20d., taking per day **4d.** In payment of John Coraunt and his boy for mending and pointing the room of the steward with tiles for 8 days 8s., taking between themselves per day **12d.** In 4 quarters of lime bought for the same & for mending the lodge similarly 8s., per **quarter, 2s.** In 130 'Roftyl'' & 'Cornertyl'' bought for the same 6s. 8d. In payment of William Coraunt & his son for tiling & pointing the lodge in the park, in the main account, for 4 days, 2s. 8d., taking between themselves per day **8d.** In one quarter of lime bought for the same, 2s.

Sum 29s.

Cost of the mills

In one sail-rod bought for 'le Northmell'' with carriage of the same, 6s. 8d. In 600 feet of boards to be sawn for roofing the mill aforesaid 5s., per 100, **10d.** In iron nails bought for fixing the said boards on the mill, 5s. In 6 iron hoops bought with nails for banding the sail-rod of the mill, 3s. In one cart hired for 1 day to carry the boards and 1 sail-rod from the timber of the lord for the second mill, 18d. In 1 beam bought for 'le Nortmell'' [*sic*], 3s. In payment of John Hokkelee hired for 27 days to erect the said rods and to place them in the mills, & to board up & repair divers defects of the same, 13s. 6d., taking per day **6d.** In payment of John Neel & Walter Hamelyn hired for 20 days to repair and erect the said mills, because thrown down by the tempest, 13s. 4d., taking between themselves per day **8d.** In expenses made about the re-establishment of the mill called 'le Northmell', 18d.

Sum 52s. 6d.

Mowing

In mowing the meadows by task-work, nothing accounted this year, because by the works without. In 42 acres 3 roods of meadow tedded, 21⅜d., per **acre ½d.** In the custom of the customary tenants for their 'madram', 12d. For the making and collecting of the said hay, nothing, because by the works without. In the expenses of the customary tenants coming with their 2 carts for 1 day by custom 6d., per cart **3d.**

Sum 3s. 3⅜d.

Wages and payments

In the wages of Simon Crowe, bailiff, yearly, 60s. 8d. Payment to the same for his clothes yearly, 10s. And for the footwear of the same during the same [*time*], 6s. 8d. In the wages of John Godard', hayward, yearly, 60s. 8d. In the wages of Walter Godard', keeper of the little park, by the precept of Thomas Tyrel, 30s. 4d. yearly, per day **1d.** In the wages of the clerk making the accounts yearly, 10s. [In the wages of Walter Woklyn, collector of the rents [tolls *interlined*] & perquisites of the Court of the borough, by custom yearly, 6s. 8d., *added in a different hand*].

Sum 9li. 5s.

Cost of the park

In 150 perches of hedge made in the park of Southfrith', 12s. 6d., per perch **1d.**, in addition to old underwood.

Sum 12s. 6d.

Expenses of the steward with external wages

In the wages of John Bienge, steward, for one whole year, 40s. In the expenses of John Bienge, steward, being here on many occasions to hold court this year, 23s. 11d. by 10 bills sealed. In the expenses of Thomas Tyrel', being here for 3 days & 3 nights to superintend the manor, together with the expenses of Lord Hugh de Badwe, knight, & Lord John Foxlee, knight, in all the expenses, 43s., by 1 tally not sealed. In carrying money to London on 3 occasions, 6s.

Sum 112s. 11d.

Payment of money

Paid to Thomas Tyrel', steward of Lady Isabel, daughter of the King of England — 85li. 6s. 8d., by five quittances sealed by the seal of the said Thomas.

Sum 85li. 6s. 8d.

[Sum of all expenses and payments 110li. 18s. 7¼d. *added in a different hand*].

[And he owes — 10li. 19s. 8¾d., whereof is allowed 30s. 4d. of the wages of Walter Godard by receipt of the steward. And 6s. 8d. of the fee of the clerk making the accounts. And thus he owes clear 9li. 2s. 8¾d., *all in a different hand*]

[*dorse*]

[*Three lines illegible, by comparison with the other accounts they relate to corn from the farm of the mills*].

[*Wheat*][1]

He answers for 10 quarters 5 bushels 3 pecks of wheat & 10 quarters 5 bushels [3 pecks *interlined*] of multure received from the farm of the said mills, that is to say, 'Cherchemell'' & 'Northmell'', thus demised [*illegible*] this year, because by any other way they could not be demised, & not more because the mill called 'le North mell'' stood empty for 6 weeks, because it was destroyed by the tempest.

Sum 22 quarters 6 bushels — And sold within — And nothing remains.

[*Geese*][1]

And for 4 from the rents of the term of Saint Michael — Sum 4 — And sold within — [And nothing remains].[1]

[*Capons*][1]

He answers for 26 from the rents of the term of the Nativity of the Lord. And for 1 received of John Alman, tanner, for using [his craft].* And for 1 received from the rent of Richard Latonner' at the same term. And for 1 from the chevage of William Stephene at the same term. And for 1 of Thomas Herde, tanner, for using his craft outside the borough.

Sum 30 — And sold within — And nothing remains.

[1] Illegible, words supplied.

[*Hens*][1]

He answers for 2 of the term of the Nativity of the Lord — Sum 2 — And sold within — And nothing remains.

[*Eggs*][1]

He answers for 285 received of the rents at the feast of Easter.

Sum 285

Thence in deduction of 3 virgates of land, whereof **1** sometime of John Punt & Hugh Punt, **1 virgate** formerly of Richard Herberd' & William Shymmyng', & **1 virgate** sometime of William Maschal & Amice Alein, because [*illegible*], whereof received from the farm as within, 90 eggs, for each virgate **30 eggs.** In selling as within 195 eggs.

Sum as above — And balances.

[*Garden*][1]

For the produce of the garden nothing paid here, because apple and pear-trees in the garden were entirely torn up by the wind this year & sold within as appears.

[*Arrows*][1]

He answers for 7 received from the rents yearly of the term of Easter.

Sum 7 — And sold as within — And balances.

Cumin

He answers for 1 pound of cumin from the rents of the term of Easter — The sum appears — And sold within — And balances.

Ploughshares

He answers for 8 from the rents of the term of Saint Boltoph. Sum 8 — And sold within. [And balances].[1]

Customary making of malt

He answers for the making of 23 quarters 2 bushels of malt arising from the issue of 7¾ virgates at the feast of the Nativity of the Lord, whereof each virgate will make **3 quarters** of malt or will give **3d.** per quarter by custom.

Sum 23 quarters 2 bushels.

Thence in deduction of the 3 virgates of land aforesaid for the abovesaid reason, the making of 9 quarters of malt. In selling as within the making of 14 quarters 2 bushels of malt.

Sum as above — And balances.

Customary ploughing, value of ploughing per acre **4d.**

He answers for the ploughing of 186 acres arising from 7¾ virgates of land in the seasons of winter, Lent & fallow, whereof each virgate will plough at each season **8 acres.**

Sum 186 acres.

Thence in deduction of the 3 virgates of land abovesaid for the abovesaid reason, the ploughing of 72 acres of land. In selling as within 114 acres.

Sum as above — And balances.

[1] Illegible, words supplied.

Winter & summer [sic][1] *works, value of the work* **½d.**

He answers for 1472½ works arising from the customary tenants holding 7¾ virgates of land between the feast of Saint Michael & the feast of the Nativity of Saint John the Baptist during 38 weeks, whereof each virgate will do each week during the same time 5 works, except on feast days falling on their work days ; and their work days are Monday, Tuesday, Wednesday, Thursday, & Friday. And the works of each virgate are **190 works.** And for 684 works arising from 9 akermen during the same time, whereof each holds 10 acres of land & will do weekly **2 works.** And the works of each are **76 works.** And for 418 works arising from 11 coterells during the same time, whereof each will do weekly **1 work.** And the works of each are **38 works.**

Sum 2574½ works.

Whereof in deduction of the works of the 3 virgates of land abovesaid for the aforesaid reason 570 works. In allowance of the 4¾ virgates of land remaining for working for their 'Gauelerthe' at the 3 seasons, that is to say, wheat, oats & fallow, above charged, 285 works, of each virgate for the same ploughing **60 works,** for the acre **2½ works.** For the allowance of the same for the 4 feast weeks during the same time, that is to say, the fortnight of the Nativity of the Lord, Easter week & Pentecost week, 95 works, And in allowance of the same during 23 feast days falling on their working days during the same time, that is to say, the feast of Saint Luke the Evangelist, All Saints, Saint Nicholas the Bishop on Mondays, All Souls, Saint Clement, the feast of Saint Andrew the Apostle, the feast of Saint Thomas the Apostle, the feast of the Conversion of Saint Paul, Cathedra of Saint Peter, the feast of the Invention of the Holy Cross on Tuesdays, the feast of Saint Martin, the feast of the Conception of the Blessed Mary, the feast of the Purification of the Blessed Virgin Mary on Wednesdays, the feast of Saints Simon & Jude, the feast of Saint Katherine, the feast of Saint Matthew the Apostle, the feast of Saint Augustus on Thursdays, [the feast of the Ascension of the Lord, the feast of Corpus Christi *interlined*], Good Friday, the feast of Saint George the Martyr, the feast of Saint John before the Latin Gate & the feast of Saint Barnabas the Apostle on Fridays, 108¾ works, that is to say, for each day each virgate, **1 work.** In deduction of 2 akermen's tenements, namely, of John Peyt & John Koc, because in the hand of the lord, and thence he answers for the farm within, during the same time 152 works. In allowance of 7 akermen remaining for working during the 4 feast weeks abovenamed, 56 works. In deduction of the works of 1 coterell, namely, 'Bretonneslond'', because in the hand of the lord, & he answers for the farm within, 38 works. And in allowance of the works of 10 coterells remaining for working during the aforesaid 4 feast weeks, 40 works. In erecting with timber the grange destroyed by the tempest & similarly fixing & putting secure the bindings & tiles within the manor of divers houses after the tempest, 72 works. In 60 perches of hedge made in the great park, 160 works. In hedges made around the 'le Parkmad'', 40 works. In the repair of the fence around 'le Parkmad'' destroyed by the tempest in places, 30 works. [5d. *written in margin*]. In selling as within 917¾ [works *interlined*]. In selling on the account 10 works.

Sum as above — And balances.

Summer works, value of the work **1d.**

He answers for 418½ works arising from the customary tenants of 7¾ virgates of land between the feast of the Nativity of Saint John the Baptist & the first day of the month of August, during 5 weeks & 2 days both for working this year, by dominical letter b, whereof each virgate of land will do each week 10 works during the abovenamed 5 weeks unless feast days shall occur on these days. And for 99 works arising from 9 akermen during the same time, whereof each will do during a whole week, **2 works.** And for 55 works arising from 11 coterells during the same time, whereof each will do during a whole week **1 work.** And for 30 works arising from 6 customary tenants called cotmen during the same time, whereof each will do during a whole week **1 work,** &

[1] Should read 'winter works' only.

will not work at another time of the year, except in Autumn as within, at the value of each work **1d.** And for 1 work arising from Richard Aylmar' for mowing the hay of the lord.

603½ works

Whereof in deduction of the 3 virgates of land aforesaid for the reason abovesaid, 162 works, to each **54 works.** In allowance of 4¾ virgates of land remaining for working for 5 feast days falling during the same time on their working days, that is to say, the feast of Saint James the Apostle on Monday, the feast of Saint Peter the Apostle & the feast of Saint Margaret on Wednesdays, the feast of the Translation of Saint Thomas the Martyr on Thursday, & the feast of Saint Mary Magdalene on Friday, [47]½[1] works, for each virgate each day **2 works.** In deduction of two akermen's tenements, namely of John Peyt & John Cok', because in the hands of the lord as above, 22 works. In deduction of the works of 1 coterell, namely 'Bretonneslond'', for the abovesaid reason, 5 works. In allowance of the said 4¾ virgates of land for the mowing of 42 acres 3 roods of meadow in 'Custumad'', whereof each virgate of land mows 9 acres, by custom 85½ works, for the mowing of each acre, **2 works.** In allowance of the same for making, collecting & making into cocks the said hay & all the hay of the demesne meadows with the other customary tenants as within, 38 works, to each virgate by custom **8 works.** In allowance of the aforesaid 7 akermen, 10 coterells and 6 cotmen remaining for working for helping in making & collecting the hay in 4 meadows mown by the customary tenants holding parcels [*illegible*] of customary land, 92 works, to each of them **4** works by custom. In allowance of the same & the said 4¾ virgates for helping to collect & make the hay of 4½ acres of meadow in 'Panphylonnesmad'' & not more, because all other meadows have been sold in grass this year, 13½ works. In selling as within 138 works.

Sum as above — And balances.

Autumn works

He answers for 651 works arising from the customary tenants holding 7¾ virgates of land between Lammas Day and the feast of Saint Michael, during 8 weeks 2 days, both for working this year, by dominical letter B, whereof each will do weekly 10 works during the abovesaid 5 days for working, unless feast days shall occur on these days. And for 153 works arising from 9 akermen during the same time, whereof each will do weekly **2 works.** And for 93½ works arising from 11 coterells during the same period, whereof each will do weekly **1 work.** And for 51 works arising from 6 cotmen during the same time, whereof each will do weekly **1 work,** at the value of each work **1d.**

Sum 948½ works.

Whereof in deduction of the 3 virgates of land abovesaid for the aforesaid reason, 252 works, for each virgate 84 works. In allowance of the works of the 4¾ virgates of land remaining for working during 7 feast days falling on their working days during the same time, that is to say, the feast of the Assumption of the Blessed Virgin Mary & the feast of the Decollation of Saint John the Baptist on Mondays, the feast of Saint Lawrence, the feast of Saint Bartholomew the Apostle, the feast of the Exaltation of the Holy Cross, the feast of Saint Matthew the Apostle on Wednesdays & the feast of the Nativity of the Blessed Virgin Mary on Thursday, 66½ works, each virgate for each day **2 works.** In deduction of the works of the aforesaid 2 akermen, that is to say, John Peyt & John Cok, for the reason abovesaid, 34 works. In deduction of the works of 1 coterell, that is to say, 'Bretonneslond'' aforesaid, for the reason aforesaid, 8½ works. In selling within 588½ works.

Sum as above — And balances.

Meadow

He answers for 26 acres 1 rood of meadow in 'Northmad'' except **1 acre 1 rood** which John Bienge holds at farm, 32 acres in 'Parkmad'', 4½ acres in 'Panfylonnesmad',' 12 acres in 'Brodefen' & 21 acres of meadow in 'Shepecotemad''.

Sum 95 acres 1 rood.

[1] Illegible, number supplied.

Whereof in the expense of 2 'hakeneys' of Simon Crowe, bailiff, & John Godard', hayward, at the time of grass, 1 acre — And the mowing by the customary tenants by custom of 42 acres 3 roods. In selling as above the herbage of 51½ acres [*some words erased*].

Sum as above — And balances.

Hay

He answers for the hay of 42 acres 3 roods of meadow mown.

42 acres 3 roods.

Whereof in tithe, the hay of 4 acres 1 rood. In selling as within the hay of 35 acres.

Sum 39 acres 1 rood — And there is expended the hay of [*illegible*] acres and a half of meadow [*illegible*] the steward & [*illegible*]

Faggots

He answers for 6340 faggots made in the park of 'Southfrith'' & in the little park.
Sum 6340
Whereof paid in tithe 640 — In selling as within 5700.

Sum as above — And balances.

[1]Memorandum of ½ virgate of land called 'Cocates', sometime of Richard Herberd', & now demised to John Terry for 8s. yearly, not contained in this roll.

[And of 1 coterell's land, sometime of William Heldere, in the hand of the lord & at farm to John Monde for 3s. yearly, not contained in this roll *all struck through,* because within *interlined*].

And of ½ virgate of land, sometime of William Mascal, demised to John Godard', as in this account-roll.

And of 1 cottage [called Gaces *struck through*], formerly of Richard Ailmar', which Gace holds by works & [*word erased*] services, not well maintained.

And of ½ virgate of land sometime of Avice Alein demised to John Godard' for 10s. yearly, as in this account-roll

And of 1 virgate of land, sometime of John Punt & Hugh Punt, thus demised to John Godard' for 20s., as in this account.

And of ½ virgate of land, sometime Shymmynges, demised to John Crakeman for 16s. 6d. yearly, as in this account. [And in the year ended the same for 19s. *interlined*].

Memorandum

And of ½ virgate of land, sometime Smythes [formerly Aleen *interlined*], demised to John Wryghte for 13s. [3 *struck through,* 4 *interlined*] d., not contained in this account.

And of ½ virgate of land, sometime of Thomas Waltham demised to Robert Trubbok', for 10s. yearly, not contained in this account. [And in the year ended for 18s. for a term of 9 years *interlined*].

Memorandum

Of 1 akerman's land, sometime of John Peyt, demised to Robert Trubbok' for [5s. 6d. *struck through,* 7s. *interlined*] yearly, whereof in this account **5s. 6d.** [And in the year ended for 12s. to Robert atte Grene *interlined*].

Of 1 akerman's land, sometime of John Cok', demised to John Abraham for 5s. 6d., as in this account.

Of 1 akerman's land, sometime of [*blank*] Grene, demised to John son of Thomas [4 works *struck through*] Godard' for 5s. yearly, not contained in this account.

Of 1 coterell's land, sometime 'Bretonneslond'', demised to John Heldere for [*blank*].

[1] Remainder of roll added in a different hand.

Of 1 coterell's land, sometime of William Heldere, at farm to John Monde for 3s. yearly, not contained in this account.

Walter Hardye holds 5 acres of bond land of a half virgate, sometime Smythes 2s. 6d.
John Heldere for 4½ acres of the said tenement for 2s. 3d.
John Nok' 1 acre of the said tenement for 6d.
John Godard 3 acres 2s. [Smyth *added in margin in a different hand*].
John Roger 2 acres 12d.
William Bakere for 1 acre of meadow for 4s.
Sum 12s. 3d.

BAILIFF'S ACCOUNT, 1377-78

Thaxstede

Account of John Neel, bailiff there, from the feast of Saint Michael the Archangel in the first year of the reign of King Richard the second after the conquest until on the Morrow of the said feast then next following in the second year of the aforesaid King, that is to say, for one whole year.

Arrears

The same answers for 58li. 5s. 2d. from the arrears of the last account there of the year preceding.

Sum — 58li. 5s. 2d.

Rents of assize & external rents

And for 4li. 5s. 2½d. from the rents of assize there at the term of the Nativity of the Lord. And for 105s. 8½d. from the rents there at Easter term. And for 4li. 2s. 11¾d. from the rents there at the term of the Nativity of Saint John the Baptist. And for 107s. 4¾d. from the rents there at the term of Saint Michael. And for 3s. 1¾d. received from 'Wardepans' yearly at the term of 'Hokeday'. And for 1d. from the new rent of William Tyle at the term of Saint Michael. And for 1d. from the new rent of John Blak' for 1 piece of ground taken from the highway at the 4 terms. And for ¼d. from the increase of the rent of William Saucer' for 1 piece of bond meadow purchased from Nicholas atte Hyde in 'Lorymerescroft' at the term of Saint Michael. And for ¼d. from the increase of the rent of William Drought for ½ acre of meadow purchased from John Saucer'. And for ½d. from the increase of the rent for 1 piece of bond meadow purchased from William Botild' at the terms of Easter & Saint Michael. And for ½d. from the new rent of Walter Abraham for 1 piece taken from the highway at 'Richemondesgrene' at the term of Saint Michael. And for ½d. from the increase of the rent of John Clerc for 1 piece of pasture lying in 'Wynterwellemed'' at the terms of Easter & Saint Michael. And for 2d. from the new rent of John Benge for a certain purpresture thus demised in the high road to 'Donmowe' at the head of 'Middelrowe' next the messuage of the said John, yearly at the terms of Easter & Saint Michael. And for ½d. from the increase of the rent of William Cokere for 1 rood of meadow & 1 acre of land which he purchased from John Peyt, bondman of the lord, at the terms of Easter & Saint Michael. And for ½d. from the new rent of John Gace for half an acre of land in 'Asshfeld'', which fell to John, son of Richard Godard, bondman of the lord, by inheritance, to hold to himself & his issue (*sequele*) by the rod, this being the 8th year. And for ½d. from the increase of the rent of Nicholas Cetard', bondman of the lord, for 1 acre of meadow purchased by charter from Thomas Bray, yearly at the 2 terms, this being the 7th year. And for 1d. from the new rent of Thomas Shethere for having 1 postern gate outside the close of the said Thomas in the lord's field, yearly at the 2 terms, this being the 7th year. And for ½d. from the increase of the rent of Nicholas Cetard' for 1 acre of free land purchased from Bartholomew Chamberleyn, yearly at the 2 terms, this being the 7th year. And for 18d. from the new rent of John Kent for 1 piece of pasture in 'Newefeld'' containing 1 rood, lying next the river near 'le Shepecotebrugg'', one head abutting on the soil of the lord towards the tenement of Edmund Stubbere, to hold to himself & his heirs by the rod, yearly at the said 4 terms, this being the 6th year. And for ¼d. from the increase of the rent of John Godard', for 1½ roods of free land purchased from William Gay, yearly at the term of Saint Michael, this being the 5th year. And for 1d. from the new rent of John le Veer' for having 1 postern gate outside his close in the lord's field called 'Mochelasshfeld'', to hold to himself & his heirs by the rod, yearly at the terms of Easter & Saint Michael. And for 2s. from the new rent of John Sale for 1 croft called 'Balleyescroft' next 'Churchemull'' thus demised to the same, yearly at the usual terms, this being the 5th year. And for ½d. from the new rent rent [*sic*] of John Kent for 1 purpresture next the tenement formerly of John Shethere, containing in length 60 feet & in width at one head 2 feet & at the other head nothing, to hold to himself & his heirs of the lord by the rod at the will of the lord, saving the right of anyone, yearly at the said terms, this being the 2nd year.

Sum — 19li. 8s. 10d.

Unfixed rents

And for 16d. from 4 geese of the rents at the term of [Saint] Michael sold at the value per head **4d.** And for [6s. 9d. *struck through,* 9s. *interlined*] from 27 capons of the rents at the term of the Nativity of the Lord sold at the value per head [**3d.** *struck through,* **4d.** *interlined*]. And for 4d. from 2 hens of the rents at the term of the Nativity of the Lord sold at the value per head **2d.** And for 8¼d. from 165 eggs of the rents at the term of Easter sold at the value per hundred **5d.** And for 10½d. from 7 arrows of the rents of Easter term, at the value of each **1½d.** And for 7s. from 7 ploughshares of the rents at the term of Saint Botolph sold at the value of each **12d.** And for 3d. from 1 lb. of cumin of the rents of Easter term sold.

Sum — 19s. 5¾d.

Rents of assize of the borough with the tolls of the market & fairs

And for 46s. 7½d. from the rents of the borough at the term of Easter. And for 46s. 7½d. from the rents there at the term of Saint Michael. And for 4s. 4d. from the farm of the stalls in the market place at the terms of Easter & Saint Michael. And for 5s. from the tolls of the market at the same terms. And for 6d. from the new rent of Thomas Lightfot for 1 piece of land at the eastern head of the grange of the manor. And for 16d. from the new rent of William atte Hyde for 1 piece of land from the lord's garden next his messuage. And for 4d. from the new rent of Walter Walkelyn opposite his tenement at the same terms. And for 1d. from the new rent of Walter Camberleyn for 1 purpresture next his house. And for 2d. from the new rent of John Frend' for 1 piece of land in the enclosure of the manor between the lord's grange and his house at the same terms. And for ½d. from the new rent of John Delauyle for 1 piece of land in 'Bolefordegardyn' at the same terms. And for 4d. from the new rent of William Coteler' for 1 piece of land within the manor next the granary on the eastern part. And for 4d. from the new rent of Robert Cretyng' for 1 piece of land there at the same terms. And for ¼d. from the new rent of John Latonner' for a certain footway next his garden going through a postern-gate as far as into 'Newefeld'', at the term of Saint Michael. And for 1d. from the new rent of John Frend for 1 piece of curtilage between the granary & the room of the steward, containing 40 feet in length & 8 feet in width, at the terms of Easter & Saint Michael. And for 1½d. from the new rent of William Lyon for 2 purprestures in the market-place next the eastern stile of the churchyard thus demised to him, at the same terms. And for 1d. from the new rent of Walter Camberleyn for 1 piece of land next his house at the same terms. And for 4d. from William atte Grene for 2 purprestures demised to the same at the will of the lord in the borough next his house, as the metes and bounds are divided, at the terms aforesaid. And for 6d. from the new rent of Walter Alwyne for 1 piece of land between his messuage & the great ditch leading from 'Asshfeld'' towards the bridge in the borough of the town aforesaid, as the metes are divided, thus demised to the same, at the terms aforesaid. And for 4s. from Thomas Lightfot for 1 parcel of the lord's garden below his messuage thus demised to the same, at the terms aforesaid. And for 6d. from Robert Cretyng' for 1 piece of vacant land on the south part of his dwelling thus demised at the will of the lord, at the terms aforesaid. And for 1d. from Richard Wolmar' for 1 piece of land of the soil of the manor in the high street of 'Thaxstede' thus demised at the will of the lord, at the terms aforesaid. And for ½d. from Roger atte Welde for 1 piece taken from the high street, to hold at the will of the lord, at the terms aforesaid. And for 1d. from William Loksmyth for 1 piece of land of the soil of the manor from the high street at the will of the lord, at the terms aforesaid. And for 2d. from the new rent of Walter Walkelyn for 1 purpresture containing in length 28 feet and in width 12 feet against the messuage sometime of Richard Hierd', at the terms aforesaid. And for 1d. yearly from the new rent of [Thomas *interlined in a different hand*] Broxheued' for 1 purpresture in the high street, at the term of Saint Michael. And for 1d. from the new rent of Walter Russhedale for 1 purpresture in 'Midelrowe', containing in length 30 feet & in width at one head 1 foot & at the other head half a foot, to hold to himself & his issue (*sequele*), yearly at the two terms, this being the 8th year. And for 2d. yearly of Richard Broxheued' for 1 piece of land containing in length 50 feet and in width 3 feet, lying in Great

'Asshfeld'', with entry & exit in the field aforesaid through 1 postern gate, to hold to himself & his issue by the rod, yearly at the said terms, this being the 8th year. And for 1d. from the new rent of Thomas Huberd' for 1 purpresture in 'Midelrowe', containing in length 16 feet & in width 7 feet, to hold to himself and his issue by the rod, yearly at the said 2 terms, this being the 8th year. And for 4d. from the new rent of Walter son of John Clerc for 1 purpresture there in length 24 feet & in width 12 feet, to hold to himself & his issue, yearly at the said 2 terms, this being the 8th year. And for 4d. from the new rent of John Auenant for 1 purpresture there in length 34 feet & width at one head 12 feet & at the other head 6 feet, to hold to himself & his issue by the rod, yearly at the said 2 terms, this being the 8th year. And for 1d. from the new rent of Thomas Boltere for 1 gate with exit outside his enclosure into the field of 'Newefeld'' through 1 postern gate, to hold to himself and his issue by the rod, yearly at the said 2 terms, this being the 8th year. And for 2d. from the new rent of John Kent for 1 purpresture next his tenement, in which there is a water course, containing in length 96 feet & in width 24 feet, to hold to himself & his heirs, yearly at the terms of Easter & [Saint] Michael equally, this being the 7th year. And for ½d. from the new rent of John Monde for 1 purpresture in which there is a water course next his tenement, in length 60 feet & in width at one head 29 feet & at the other head 27 feet, to hold to himself & his heirs by the rod yearly, at the terms aforesaid, this being the 7th year. And for ½d. from the new rent of John Kent for 1 purpresture between the tenement of Henry de Yerdelee & the bridge called 'Chalonneresbrugg'', containing in length 20 feet & in width 10 feet, to hold to himself & his heirs by the rod, yearly at the said 2 terms, this being the 6th year. And for 2d. from the new rent of Thomas Boltere for having entry & exit with horses & carts from the tenement of the said Thomas into the field of 'Newefeld'' over the soil of the lord from the town of 'Thaxstede' beyond the bridge called 'Shepecotebrugg'', & from the tenement of the said Thomas to a certain piece of his land lying in the said field of 'Newefeld'' as often as & whenever he shall require, to hold to himself & his heirs, yearly at the said 2 terms, this being the 6th year. And for 1d. from the new rent of Walter Russhedale for having a certain exit through 1 postern-gate from his tenement into the field of 'Shepecotefeld'', to hold to himself & his heirs by the rod, yearly at the 2 said terms, this being the 4th year. And for 2d. from the new rent of Thomas Boltere for having exit through 1 postern-gate from his tenement into the lord's field, in length 50 feet & in width 24 feet, to hold to himself & his heirs, yearly at the said terms, this being the 2nd year. And for 1d. from the new rent of Walter Clerc for having exit outside his tenement through 1 postern gate, to hold to himself & his heirs, yearly at the said terms, this being the 2nd year. [It is examined up to here *added in margin in a different hand*]. And for 3d. from the new rent of John Boyton', junior, for one piece of land in 'Newefeld'' next the tenement of the said John, containing in length 5 perches & in width at one head 1½ perches & at the other head 1 perch, to hold to himself & his heirs, with freedom of entry & exit through 1 postern-gate, by the rod, saving the right of anyone, yearly at the said terms, this being the first year. And for 2d. from the new rent of [John *struck through,* Thomas *interlined in a different hand*] Mannyng for 1 piece of land in 'Newefeld'' next the tenement of the said Thomas, containing in length 3 perches & in width 15 feet, to hold to himself & his heirs by the rod, saving the right of anyone, yearly at the said terms, this being the first year. And for 18d. from the new rent of William Pamphylon' for 1 piece of curtilage containing in length 6¾ perches & in width 1½ perches, lying in 'Bernewyk'', with freedom of entry & exit outside his own tenement, to hold to himself & his heirs, yearly at the said terms, this being the first year. And for 2d. from the new rent of Thomas May for 1 piece of land in 'Newefeld'' next his own tenement, containing in length 4 perches & in width at one head 25 feet & at the other head 1 perch, to hold to himself & his heirs, yearly at the said terms, this being the first year. And for 2d. from the new rent of William Botelmakere for 1 piece of land containing [in length *interlined*] 60 feet & in width 30 feet, lying next 'Bulfordegardyn', to hold to himself & his heirs, yearly at the said terms, this being the first year. And for 4d. from the new rent of Janyn Sawuer' for 1 piece of land lying between the lord's garden on the one part & the highway on the other part, containing in length 64 feet & in width 30 feet, to hold to himself & his heirs by the rod, saving the right of anyone, yearly at the said terms, this being the first year. And for the half part of a 1d. yearly from the new rent of Walter Foot' for 1 purpresture containing in length 14 feet & in width 3 feet, lying next his tenement, to hold to himself & his heirs, yearly at the said terms, this being the first year.

Sum — 116s. 3¼d.

Farm of land

And for 20s. from the farm of one virgate of land, sometime of John Punt and Hugh Punt, thus demised to John Godard', yearly at the 4 terms. And for 16s. from the farm of 40 acres of land sometime 'Doketteslond'' thus demised to John Bienge at the will of the lord, yearly at the said 4 terms. And for 12s. from the farm of 16 acres of land & 1 acre of meadow, sometime of Pamphilon', thus demised to John Danyel, at the same terms. And for 6s. 10d. from the farm of 20½ acres of demesne land in 'Northfeld'' thus demised to John Bienge, at the same terms. And for 5s. from Master Thomas Vfford', vicar there, for the farm of 1 croft sometime of Nicholas atte Hyde, yearly, thus demised to the same at the will of the lord, at the said terms. And for 2s. 2d. from the new farm of Thomas Woubourne for 1 croft of land with 1 piece of curtilage called 'Rollecoescroft' thus demised to the same for the term of his life, yearly at the said terms. And for 7s. 6d. from John Clerc for the farm of 13 acres 3 roods of demesne land in 'Boxstede' with 1 piece called 'Alsichewelle' thus demised to the same, yearly at the said terms. And for 2s. 8d. from the farm of 5 acres of demesne land there thus demised to Margery Dessex [formerly of John Smyth' *interlined*] at the will of the lord, yearly at the said terms. And for 4s. from the farm of 5 roods of meadow in 'Northmad' thus demised to John Bienge, at the same terms. And for 14s. from John Terry for the farm of a half virgate of land called 'Cokattes', sometime of Richard Herberd', thus demised to the same [for the term of 9 years, this being the 7th year, yearly at the said terms *struck through*, & his heirs saving the right of anyone, this being the first year, as appears in a court held there the 7th day of the month of October in the first year *interlined*]. And for 19s. from John Crakeman for the farm of a half virgate of land, sometime of Shymyng', thus demised to the same for the term of 9 years, this being the 7th year. And for 12s. from Robert atte Grene for the farm of the tenement, formerly of John Peyt, akerman, thus demised to the same for the term of 9 years, this being the 7th year. And for 3s. from John Heldere for the farm of the tenement called 'Bretonneslond'' of coterell tenure thus demised to the same this year. For **15d.** from the farm of 1 croft of land, sometime of John Ballie, next the mill, nothing here because rented to John Sale, as appears above, paid within. And for 3s. from John Haftere for the farm of 6 acres of demesne land in 'Boxstede', formerly in the hands of William Fromond, thus demised to the same this year. And for 11s. from John Godard' for the farm of a half virgate of land, sometime of Avise Aleein, this year. And for 12s. from the same John for a half virgate of land, sometime of William Marschal, this year. And for 18s. from Robert Trubbok' for the farm of a half virgate of land, sometime of Thomas Waltham, formerly of Walter Scamp', for the term of 9 years, this being the 7th year. And for 14s. from John Wryghte for the farm of a half virgate of land, sometime of John Aleein, for the term of 9 years, this being the 7th year. And for 8s. from John Abraham for the farm of 1 akerman's land, sometime of John Cook', for the term of 9 years, this being the 7th year. And for 8s. from John son of Thomas Godard for the farm of 1 akerman's land, sometime of John Grene, thus demised to the same for the term of 9 years, this being the 7th year. And for 3s. from John Monde for the farm of 1 coterell's bond land, sometime of William Heldere, thus demised to the same, yearly. And for 2s. from John son of Adam Herry for the farm of 1 cottage with a certain curtilage, sometime of Richard Daubere, in the hands of the lord by the name of escheat, demised for the term of 20 years, this being the 8th year, yearly at the 4 terms. And for 4s. from John Smartman for the farm of a half akerman's land, sometime of Matilda Haftere, for the term of 9 years, this being the 7th year. And for 4s. from William Tyle for 1 coterell's land called 'Rammes', formerly in the hands of Thomas Fischerre, thus demised to the same for the term of 9 years, this being the 7th year, yearly at the said terms. And for 23s. 6d. from John Yerdelee for the farm of 1 piece of land containing 159 acres of the lord's demesne in 'Northfeld'' thus demised to the same for the term of 9 years, this being the 3rd year, yearly at the said terms. [Examined up to here *added in margin in a different hand*]. [And for [*blank*] from John Terry for the farm of 1 messuage & a half virgate of land called 'Cokatteslond'' thus demised to the same for the term of 7 years, this being the first year: for which present tenure the same John is to pay for the works & other services against the extent *struck through, because above under the name Herberd' interlined*].

Sum — 11li. 14s. 8d.

New farms of the issue of the demesne

And for 37li. 1d. from the farm of demesne lands, meadows & pasture demised to divers men, as appears by the parcels annexed hereto.

Sum — 37li. 1d.

Revenues of the manor

And for 37s. 6d. from 1500 faggots in 'Oldefrith'' and 'Southfrith'' sold to divers men, at the value per hundred **2s. 6d.** And for 6s. 8d. from 10 cart-loads of wood in 'Oldefrith'' sold to divers men, at the value per cart-load **8d.** And for 2s. from 3 cart-loads of wood in 'Southfrith'' next 'le Trenck'' sold to Ralph Goseprest.

Sum — 46s. 2d.

Agistment of the parks

From the agistment of divers beasts sent out into 'Shouthfrith'' [*sic*] nothing this year on account of the multitude of the beasts of the chase there, by witness of the Receiver on the account. And for 13s. 4d. from the agistment of divers beasts sent out into the little park there, as appears by the parcels annexed hereto.

Sum — 13s. 4d.

Sale of pasture

From the sale of pasture nothing here, because it is contained among the items of the new farms of demesne, as in the schedule annexed hereto. And for 43s. 6d. from the hay of 9 acres [1 rood *interlined*] of meadow sold to divers men, that is to say, to Walter Spowne, **12s. 6d.**, John Serle, **8s.**, John Hert, **18s.** Walter Bakere, **3s.**, & William Reymond, **3s.** And for 20s. from the haymaking of 32 acres of meadow sold to John Harry. For **2s.** from the haymaking of 4 acres of meadow in 'Pamphilonesmade' nothing here, because sold in herbage with the other crops, as appears in the schedule hereto annexed. For **12d.** from the haymaking of 3 acres 1 rood of meadow in 'Brodefan' nothing for the reason aforesaid.

Sum — 64s. 6d.

Sale of works

And for 2s. 9¾d. received from the making of 11 quarters 2 bushels of malt of barley from the revenues of the customary tenants sold, per quarter **2d.** And for 30s. from 90 ploughings from the issues of the customary tenants sold at the value per ploughing **4d.** And for 18s. 3d. from 438 winter works from the issues of the same sold at the value per work **½d.** And for 13s. 10¼d. from 166 summer works & a quarter part from the issues of the same sold at the value per work **1d.** And for 39s. 1½d. from 469½ autumn works from the revenues of the same sold at the value per work **1d.**

Sum — 104s. ½d.

Sale of corn

And for 31s. 8d. from 10 quarters of wheat from the farm of the mills, whereof **5 quarters** at the value per quarter **3s. 4d.**, and 5 quarters at the value per quarter **3s.** And for 26s. 8d. from 10 quarters of multure from the farm of the said mills sold at the value per quarter **2s. 8d.**

Sum — 58s. 4d.

Perquisites of the courts

And for 19li. 15s. from the perquisites of 16 courts with leet held there this year.

Sum — 19li. 15s.

Sales on the account

And for 5s. 4d. from divers things sold on the account, as appears without.

Sum — 5s. 4d.

Sum total of receipts with arrears — 167li. 11s. 2½d. — it is proved.

Allowances & deductions of rents

Thereof he reckons in deduction of the rent of the tenement, sometime Pamphilons, because in the hands of the lord & at farm above, yearly at the 4 terms, 4s. 4d. And in deduction of the rent of 1 croft, sometime of Nicholas atte Hyde, in the hands of the lord, yearly, 3s. And in deduction of the rent of 1 piece of land, sometime of William Dauy & Robert Carpenter, in the hands of the lord, & there is the wall (*fouea*) for enclosing the lord's garden from 'Bulfordegardyn' unto the piece of land sometime of Pykel, yearly at the terms of Easter & Saint Michael, 16½d. [from the allowance of the reeve *interlined*]. And in deduction of the rent of 1 piece of land of Osebert Anable & Geoffrey Miller (*Molendinar'*), lying in the highway towards 'Berdf(ield)', in the hands of the lord & lying vacant, at the same terms, 6d. [of the allowance of the borough *interlined*]. And in deduction of the rent of 1 piece of land, sometime of Geoffrey Ilger', Robert Cappe & Philip Smith (*Fabri*), because in the hands of the lord, lying vacant, at the same terms, 10d. [of the allowance of the borough *interlined*]. And in deduction of the rent of 1 stall, sometime of Thomas Montioye, in the hands of the lord, lying vacant in the borough, at the same terms, 2d. [allowance of the borough *interlined*]. And in deduction of the rent of 1 croft of land containing 1½ acres, sometime of John Ballie, in the hands of the lord & at farm above, yearly at the 4 terms, 2s. 2d. And in deduction of the rent of 1 stall, sometime of Andrew Campyon', of 1 stall sometime of William atte Noke & William Homan, of 1 stall sometime of Henry Hendys, of 1 stall sometime of Adam Seyntalbons & Nicholas atte Hyde, of 1 stall sometime of Richard Horell, of 1 stall sometime of William atte Hel, of 1 stall sometime of Jane de Berdf(eld) and William Tannere, of 3 stalls of John Pullecoo, of 1 stall sometime of Edmund Danyel, of 1 stall sometime of Richard Arnold' & Roger Huberd', of 1 stall sometime of John Pontfreyt, of 1 stall sometime of John Hydeman & William son of John Shethere, & of 1 stall sometime of John Spayne & Thomas Flatbacon', in the hands of the lord by default of the tenants, during the same time, 2s. 6d., that is to say, for each stall, **2d.** [of the allowance of the borough *interlined*]. And in deduction of the rent of 1 cottage with curtilage, sometime of Richard Daubere, in the hands of the lord by the name of escheat & at farm above to John son of Adam Herry, yearly, 4d. And in deduction of the rent of 1 coterell's land, sometime Rames, in the hands of the lord, this being the 7th year, at farm to William Tyle as above, yearly, 12d. And in deduction of the rent of 1 croft of land with 1 curtilage, sometime Rullecos, because in the hands of the lord & at farm above to Thomas Wobourne, yearly, 4d., this being the 7th year. [Item in default of the external rents above charged, because it is unknown when they ought to be levied, as had been examined throughout the rents of every tenant by Thomas a Hildeburgh', whereof the particulars named are entered in a certain new rental, yearly, 24s. 11½d. *struck through*].

Sum — 16s. 6½d.

Costs of the houses

And in nails purchased for the repair of 2 entrances of the screened off part of the hall (*host' del tresauns*), 2d. And in 1 iron chain purchased for binding 1 'poste' below 'le Garyte' next the gate of the manor broken off, 8d. And in payment of 1 tiler for 1 day tiling all defects of the kitchen, 4d. And in payment of 2 carpenters for 1 day repairing the bridge towards 'Shepecotemad'', 8d., with 2 small oaks felled in 'Oldefryth'' for the said work.

Sum — 22d.

Necessities

And in payment of 2 carpenters for 12 days felling timber & thence making 2 new bays (*bayos*), whereof **1** at 'Bulfordebrugg'' & **1** at 'Serlesbrugg'', for draining the cisterns of water in divers places of the park, 8s., to either per week **2s.** And in making 1500 faggots in 'Oldefrith'' & 'Southfrith'' [12s. 6d. *struck through*, 10s. *interlined*], per hundred [10d. *struck through*, 8d. *interlined*].

Sum — 18s.

Costs of the mills

And paid for plastering the mill house newly built, as in the preceding account, in all, 3s. And in 1,000 'Lathnail'' purchased for the said house, 16d. And in 100 'dorenail' & 'Wyndowenail' purchased for the work of the said house, 6d. And in 1 iron chain purchased for binding the sail-rod of 'Cherchemelne' with nails for the same, 6d. And in the repair of the rind (*del ryne*) & spindle (*fusill'*) of the mill of 'Chirchmulle' with the iron part purchased for the same, 20d. And in 4 'doullegges' and 2 iron chains for the mill rod of 'Chirchemulle', 12d. And in the cleansing of the pond around the mill of 'Chirchemull'' by 1 man on 4 days, 16d.

Sum — 9s. 4d.

Mowing of the meadows

And in mowing 17 acres — of meadow nothing here, because by the works of the customary tenants as without. And in tedding the grass thereof by task-work, 8½d., per acre, **½d.** And in the custom of the customary tenants mowing the lord's meadows for their ram, 12d. And in making the hay nothing here, because by the works as without. And in the custom of 5 carts of the customary tenants carrying the hay of the lord from the meadows to the grange for 1 day, 15d., to each cart by custom, **3d.**

Sum — 2s. 11½d.

Wages & payments

And in the wages of John Neel, bailiff there, yearly, 60s. 8d., taking per day **2d.** And in the payment & the clothes of the same during the same time, because he has taken nothing from the livery of the lord, 16s. 8d. And in the wages of Thomas Warewik', collector of the rents & of the court of the borough, this year, 6s. **8d.**

Sum — 4li. 4s.

Costs of the parks

And in the payment of 1 man for 3 days repairing the fence next the gate of the great park called 'Wodegate', 12d., per day, **4d.**

Sum — 12d.

Annuity

And paid to Hugh Huse of a certain annuity granted to him by the lord for the term of the life of the same Hugh, to be received of this manor yearly at the terms of Easter & Saint Michael equally, by charter of the same lord, according to the warranty of the account of the 3rd year preceding settled & the acquittance of the same Hugh on this account paid, 40s.

Sum — 40s.

Payment of the farm

And paid to Lord (*domino*) Richard Lescrop' for the farm of ¼ part of the manor appertaining to Lord Tibbetot from the term of [*Saint*] Michael in the 51st year, 13li. 6s. 8d., by 1 acquittance of the same Richard paid on the account. And paid to the same Lord Richard for the farm aforesaid from Easter term this year, 13li. 6s. 8d., by 1 acquittance of the same Richard paid on the account.

Sum — 26li. 13s. 4d.

External expenses & expenses of the auditors

In money paid for the tax of a 15th, nothing this year. And in the expenses of Thomas de Hildeburghe being here for 1 night to enter items in the month of February, 6d. And in the expenses of the same for making the view of the account in the month of May, 7d.

Sum — 13d.

Payments of money

And paid to William Aylmer, Receiver of Clare, by the hand of the accountant — 69li. 19s. — by 4 tallies, whereof the first contains **19li.**, the second **17li. 9s.**, the third **17li.**, and the fourth **16li. 10s.** [Received *added in the margin in a different hand*]. And to the same Receiver by hand of the same at the end of the account — 4li. — without tally. [Received *added in the margin in a different hand*].

Sum — 73li. 19s.

Sum total of allowances and payments — 109li. 7s. 1d. And he owes 58li. 4s. 1½d.

Whereof are respited 9li. 19s. 8d. from the deduction of rents disallowed this year & the 7 years previously elapsed, that is to say, **24s. 11½d.** yearly, until the Rental be examined, whereof from the charge of John Neel **4li. 7s. 4¼d.** And to the same 10s. from 3 capons & 1 ploughshare accounted for in deduction of the rent similarly disallowed this year & the 4 years previously elapsed, that is to say, **12d.** yearly for the said capons & **12d.** for the aforesaid ploughshare, until as above, whereof from the charge of John Neel, **7s.**

Sum respited, 10li. 9s. 8d. And he owes clear 4[7li.][1] 14s. 5½d.

Whereof to

John Godard formerly bailiff — 8li.

John Neel the accountant — 39li. 14s. 5½d., whereof is assigned to be paid to Richard Scrop' for the term of [*Saint*] Michael ending this account, **13li. 6s. 8d.**

And thus there remains — 26li. 7s. 9½d.

[*dorse*]

Wheat

The same answers for 4 quarters from the farm of the mill of 'Northmelne' thus demised this year to Thomas Miller (*Moln'*) by view of the Constable, and so much of the multure within. Nevertheless there is wont to be demised **5 quarters.** And for 6 quarters from the farm of the mill of 'Churchemelne' thus demised this year to Peter Mulnere by view of the same Constable.

Sum — 10 — quarters — And sold as within. — And balances.

Multure of the mill

And for 4 quarters of multure from the farm of the mill of 'Northmelne' thus demised this year to the aforesaid Thomas ; there is wont to be **5 quarters.** And for 6 quarters from the farm of the mill of 'Churchemelne' for the same time thus demised to the aforesaid Peter ; there is wont to be **7 quarters 4 bushels.**

Sum — 10 quarters — And sold as within. — And balances.

Geese

And for 4 from the rents there yearly at the term of Saint Michael. Sum 4 — And sold as within — And balances.

Capons

And for 26 from the rents of the tenants there at the term of the Nativity of the Lord. And for 1 capon from William Alman for licence to use the craft of tanner, at the said term. And for 1 capon from the rent of Richard Latonnere at the same term. And for 1 from the chevage of William Stephen, bondman of the lord. And for 1 capon from Thomas Hierde for licence to use the craft of tanner & to remain outside the borough, at the same term.

Sum — 30

Whereof in exoneration of the rents [because the bailiff does not know when they ought to be levied or who is held to pay, as was examined throughout the individual rents by Thomas de Hildeburghe in the month of June in the 6th year preceding, 3 *struck through*]. And in selling as within 27. And in selling on the account 3 for 12d.

Sum as above — And balances.

[1] Illegible, '7li' supplied.

Hens

And for 2 from the rents there at the term of the Nativity of the Lord. Sum 2. And sold within. — And balances.

Eggs

And for 285 eggs from the customary rents at the term of Easter. Sum 285 eggs.

Whereof in deduction of the rents of 4 virgates of land, whereof **1** virgate formerly of John Punt, **1** virgate formerly of Richard Herberd' & William Shymyng', **1** virgate sometime of William Maschal & Amice Aleyn, ½ virgate of land sometime of Walter Scamp', & ½ virgate of land sometime of John Aleein, because in the hands of the lord & at farm as within, 120 eggs, that is to say, for each virgate **30 eggs.** [And in deduction of the rent of ½ virgate of land called 'Cocatteslond'' in the hands of the lord by default of the tenant & at farm as within to John Terry, this being the first year, 15 eggs *struck through,* because above under the name Herberd *interlined*]. And in selling as within 165 eggs. Sum as above — And balances.

Arrows

And for 7 from the rents there yearly at the term of Easter. Sum 7. And sold as within — And balances.

Ploughshares

And for 8 from the rents there yearly at the term of Saint Botolph.

Sum 8

[Whereof in exoneration of the rents because it is not known when they ought to be levied or who is held to pay, as was examined by the aforesaid Thomas in the month of June in the 6th year preceding *struck through*]. And in selling as within 7. And in selling as above on the account 1 for 12d.

Sum as above — And balances.

Cumin

And for 1 pound of cumin from the rents there at Easter term. Sum 1 pound. And sold as within — And balances.

The garden

For the produce of the garden nothing here because within at farm.

Account of works

Making of malt

And for the making of 23 quarters 2 bushels of barley into malt arising from the revenues of 7¾ virgates of land at the feast of the Nativity of the Lord, whereof each virgate will make **3 quarters** of barley into malt or will give for the making of each **quarter 3d.** by custom. Sum of the making — 23 quarters 2 bushels.

Thence in deduction of the 4 virgates of land abovesaid, because in the hands of the lord & at farm as within, the making of 12 quarters of barley into malt. And in selling as within the making of [9 quarters 6 bushels *struck through,* 11 quarters 2 bushels *interlined*] of malt. Sum as above — And balances.

Customary ploughing, value of the ploughing of each acre **4d.**

And for the ploughing of 186 acres of land arising from 7¾ virgates of land at the season of winter, Lent & fallow, whereof each virgate will plough at each season **8 acres of land.**

Sum of the ploughing 186 acres.

Whereof in deduction of the ploughing of the aforesaid 4 virgates for the abovesaid reason, the ploughing of [108 *struck through,* 96 *interlined*] acres. And in selling as within the ploughing of [78 *struck through,* 90 *interlined*] acres. Sum as above — And balances.

Winter works, value of the work **½d.**

And for 1472½ works arising by custom from the customary tenants holding among themselves 7¾ virgates of land between the feast of Saint Michael & the feast of the Nativity of Saint John the Baptist, during 38 weeks for certain, whereof each virgate of land will do each week during the same time **5 works**, that is to say, Monday, Tuesday, Wednesday, Thursday & Friday, unless feast days shall fall on those days. And thus from each virgate **190 works.** And for 684 works arising from 9 akermen during the same time, whereof each holds 10 acres of land & will do weekly **2 works.** And thus from each of them **76 works.** And for 418 works arising from 11 coterells during the same time, whereof each will do each week **1 work.** And thus from each of them **38 works.**

Sum 2574½ works.

Whereof in deduction of the works of the 4 virgates of land aforesaid for the reason abovesaid 760 works. And in allowance of the works of the aforesaid 3¾ virgates of land for the ploughing of [78 *struck through* 90 *interlined*] acres of land as above at the 3 seasons by the custom called 'Gauelerthe' 225 works, that is to say, for the ploughing of each acre **2½ works.** And in allowance of the works of the same for 4 feast weeks during the same time, that is to say, the fortnight of the Nativity of the Lord, the weeks of Easter & Pentecost, 75 works. And in allowance of the works of the same for 14 feast days falling during their working days within the said time, that is to say, the Apostles Simon & Jude on Wednesday, All Souls on Monday, Saint Katherine the Virgin on Wednesday, Saint Andrew the Apostle on Monday, the Conception of the Blessed Mary on Tuesday, Saint Thomas the Apostle on Monday, the Conversion of Saint Paul on Monday, the Purification of the Blessed Mary on Tuesday, Saint Peter in Cathedra on Monday, Saint Matthew the Apostle on Wednesday, the Annunciation of the Blessed Mary on Thursday, the Invention of the Cross on Monday, the Ascension of the Lord & Corpus Christi on Thursday, 52½ works, that is to say, for each virgate each day **1** work. And in deduction of the works of 3½ akermen, that is to say, **1** John Peyt, **1** John Cook, **1** John Grene, & ½ Matilda Haftere, because in the hands of the lord & at farm as within, 266 works, for each akerman **76 works** [for each akerman 76 works *struck through*]. And in deduction of the works of the tenement of John Yongy, ½ akerman, in the hands of the lord by default of the tenant, this being the 2nd year, 38 works. And in allowance of the works of 5 akermen working during the 4 weeks abovesaid, 40 works, for each akerman **8 works.** And in deduction of the works of 2 coterells, that is to say, 1 called 'Bretonneslond'' & 1 sometime of William Helder', because in the hands of the lord & at farm as within, 76 works. And in deduction of the works of 1 coterell's land called 'Rammes', sometime of Matilda Fischere, because in the hands of the lord & at farm as within to William Tyle, 38 works. And in allowance of the works of 8 coterells working during the 4 feast weeks abovesaid by custom, 32 works. And in the making of 267 perches of new hedge around 'Southfrith'', 534 works, that is to say, per perch **2 works.** And in selling as within 438 works.

Sum as above — And balances.

Summer works, value of the work **1d.**

And for 418½ summer works arising by custom from the customary tenants holding among themselves 7¾ virgates of land between the feast of the Nativity of Saint John the Baptist & Lammas Day, during 5 weeks & 2 days for working this year; they (*qui*) will work for each virgate of land weekly **10 works** for the aforesaid 5 days for working, unless feast days shall fall on those days. And thus for each virgate 54 works. And for 99 works arising from the aforesaid 9 akermen during the same time, whereof each will do weekly **2 works.** And for 55 works arising from 11 coterells during the same time, whereof each will do weekly **1** work. And for 30 works arising from 6 cotmen during the same time, whereof each will do weekly **1** work & they will not work except, however, in Autumn. And for 1 work arising from Richard Ailmer' for making the lord's hay.

Sum 603½ works.

Whereof in deduction of the works of the aforesaid 4 virgates for the reason as above, 216 works. And in allowance of the works of the aforesaid 3¾ virgates of land for 3 feast days falling during the working days within the said time, that is to say, the Apostles Peter & Paul on Tuesday, the Translation of Saint Thomas the Martyr on Wednesday, Saint Mary Magdalene on Thursday, 22½ works. And in deduction of the works of the [aforesaid *interlined*] 3½ akermen in the hands of the lord for the reasons above, 38½ works. And in deduction of the works of the tenement of John Yonge, ½ akerman, in the hands of the lord by default of the tenant, this being the 2nd year, 5¼ works. And in deduction [of the works *interlined*] of 3 coterells abovesaid for the aforesaid reason, 15 works. And in allowance of the works of the aforesaid 3¾ virgates of land for mowing 17 acres of meadow in 'Parkmad'', 34 works, that is to say, per acre **2 works** [nevertheless each virgater will mow **9 acres**, if it be needed, by custom *interlined*]. And in allowance of the works of the same for making, collecting & making into cocks the hay of the said meadow with the help of the cotmen as within, 30 works, that is to say, for each virgater by custom **8 works**. And in allowance of the works of the aforesaid 5 akermen, 8 coterells & 6 cotmen working to make the said hay & to make [*it*] into cocks by custom, 76 works, for each of them **4 works.** And in allowance of the works of divers customary tenants for turning, removing & making the hay of 4 acres of meadow in 'Pamphilonnesmede', because not of the demesne of the manor, that is to say, from each of them daily **2 works**, nothing this year, because sold in grass as within. And in selling as within 166¼ works. [It is examined *added in margin in a different hand*].

Sum as above — And balances.

Autumn works, value of the work **1d.**

And for 651 works arising by custom from the customary tenants holding among themselves 7¾ virgates of land between Lammas Day & the feast of Saint Michael falling on Tuesday this year, that is to say, for 8 weeks & 2 days for working; they (*qui*) will work for each virgate of land weekly 10 works during the aforesaid 5 working days, unless feast days shall fall on those days. And thus for each virgate **84 works.** And for 144 works arising from 9 akermen during the same time, whereof each will do weekly **2 works**. And for 88 works arising from 11 coterells during the same time, whereof each will do weekly **1 work**. And for 48 works arising from 6 cotmen during the same, whereof each will do weekly **1 work**.

Sum 931 works.

Whereof in deduction of the works of the aforesaid 4 virgates for the reason aforesaid 336 works, that is to say, for each virgate **84 works**. And in allowance of the works of the aforesaid 3¾ virgates working for the 5 feast days falling on their working days during the time aforesaid, that is to say, Saint Lawrence on Tuesday, Saint Bartholomew the Apostle on Tuesday, the Nativity of the Blessed Mary on Wednesday, the Exaltation of the Holy Cross on Tuesday & Saint Matthew the Apostle on Tuesday, 37½ works. And in deduction of the works of the 4 akermen abovesaid, because in the hands of the lord as above, 64 works. And in deduction of the works of 3 coterells as above for the reason aforesaid, 24 works. And in selling as within 469½ works.

Sum as above — And balances.

Meadow

And for 26 acres 1 rood of meadow in 'Northmad', except 1 acre of meadow there which John Bienge holds at farm. In 'Parkmad', 32 acres. In 'Panphilonesmad'', 4 acres. In 'Brodefan', 12 acres. In 'Shepecotemad'', 21 acres.

Sum — 95 acres 1 rood.

[Thence in the sustenance of 1 horse of the bailiff this year 1 acre *struck through*]. And there are mown by the works of the customary tenants 17 acres. And in selling as within in grass, as appears by the parcels annexed hereto, 77 acres 1 rood. And in selling on the account 1 acre for 3s. 4d.

Sum as above — And balances.

Hay

And for the hay of 6 acres of meadow of the remainder. — And for the hay of 17 acres of meadow from the mowing this year.

Sum — of hay — 23 acres.

Thence in tithes, the hay of 1 acre 3 roods. And in the expenses of the horses of the Steward, the Receiver, the Auditors & others of the lord's council this year, the hay of 3 acres. And in the sustenance of the wild beasts in the park, the hay of 3 acres. And in selling as within the hay of 9 acres 1 rood.

Sum of hay — 17 acres — And there remains the hay of 6 acres of meadow.

Haymaking

And for the haymaking of 35 acres 1 rood of meadow, whereof in 'Parkmade' **32 acres** & in 'Brodefan' 3 acres 1 rood.

Sum — 35 acres 1 rood — And sold as within. And balances.

Faggots

And for 1500 faggots of this year's making, in addition to tithe.

Sum — 1500 faggots — And in selling as within. And balances.

BAILIFF'S ACCOUNT, 1380-81

Thaxstede

Account of John Godard', Bailiff there, from the feast of Saint Michael the Archangel in the 4th year of the reign of King Richard the second after the conquest until the Morrow of the said Feast then next following in the 5th year of the aforesaid King entering, that is to say, for one whole year.

Arrears

The same answers for 73li. 5s. 8¾d. from the arrears of the last account there of the preceding year.

Sum 73li. 5s. 8¾d. — it is tested.

Rents of Assize

And for 4li. 5s. 2½d. from the rents of assize there at the term of the Nativity of the Lord. And for 105s. 8½d. from the rents there at Easter term. And for 4li. 2s. 11¾d. from the rents there at the term of the Nativity of Saint John the Baptist. And for 107s. 4¾d. from the rents there at the term of Saint Michael. And for 3s. 1¾d. received from 'Wardepans' yearly at the term of 'Hokeday'. And for 1d. from the new rent of William Tile at the term of Saint Michael. And for 1d. from the new rent of John Blak' for 1 piece taken from the highway, at the 4 terms. And for ¼d. from the increase of the rent of William Saucer' for 1 piece of bond-meadow purchased from Nicholas atte Hyde in 'Lorimerescroft', at the term of Saint Michael. And for ¼d. from the increase of the rent of William Drought for ½ acre of meadow purchased from John Saucer'. And for ½d. from the increase of the rent for 1 piece of bond-meadow purchased from William Botild', at the terms of Easter & Saint Michael. And for ½d. from the new rent of Walter Abraham for 1 piece taken from the highway at 'Richemondesgrene', at the term of Saint Michael. And for ½d. from the [new *struck through,* increase *interlined*] of the rent of John Clerk' for 1 piece of pasture lying in 'Wynterwellemed'', at the terms of Easter & Saint Michael. And for 2d. from the new rent of John Benge for a certain purpresture thus demised to him in the high road towards 'Donmowe', at the head of 'Middelrowe', next the messuage of the said John, yearly at the terms of Easter & Saint Michael. And for ½d. from the increase of the rent of William Cokere for 1 rood of meadow & 1 acre of land which he purchased from John Peyt, bondman of the lord, at the terms of Easter & Saint Michael. And for ½d. from the new rent of John Gace for ½ acre of land in 'Asshefeld'' which fell to John, son of Richard Godard', bondman of the lord, by inheritance, to hold to himself & his issue (*sequele*) by the rod, this being the 11th year. And for ½d. from the increase of the rent of Nicholas Setard', bondman of the lord, for 1 acre of meadow purchased by charter from Thomas Bray, yearly at the 2 terms, this being the 10th year. And for 1d. from the new rent of [Thomas *interlined*] Shethere for having 1 postern gate outside the close of the said Thomas in the lord's field, yearly at the 2 terms, this being the 10th year. And for ½d. from the increase of the rent of Nicholas Setard' for 1 acre of free land purchased from Bartholomew Chamberlayn, yearly at the 2 terms, this being the 10th year. And for 18d. from the new rent of John Kent for 1 piece of pasture in 'Newefeld'' containing 1 rood, lying next the river near 'le Shepecotebregge', one head abutting upon the soil of the lord towards the tenement of Edward Stubbere, to hold to himself & his heirs by the rod, yearly at the said 4 terms, this being the 9th year. And for ¼d. from the increase of the rent of John Godard' for 1½ roods of free land purchased from William Gay, yearly at the term of Saint Michael, this being the 8th year. And for 1d. from the new rent of John le Veer' for having 1 postern gate outside his close in the lord's field called 'Muchelasshfeld'', to hold to himself & his heirs by the rod, yearly at the terms of Easter & Saint Michael. And for 2s. from the new rent of John Sale for 1 croft called 'Ballayescroft' next 'Churchemulle' thus demised to him, yearly at the usual terms, this being the 8th year. And for ½d. from the new rent of John Kent for 1 purpresture next the tenement formerly of John Shethere, containing 60 feet in length & in width at one head 2 feet & at the other head nothing, to hold to himself & his heirs of the lord by the rod, at the will of the lord, saving the right of anyone, yearly at the said terms, this being the 5th year. And for 2s. 7½d.

from the new rent of William Serlee for 1 acre 3 roods of demesne land lying in 'le Worthene', to hold to himself & his issue (*sequele*) by the rod, yearly at the usual terms, this being the 2nd year. And for 6s. 8d. from the new rent of John Kent for 2 acres of demesne land in 'Asshefeld'' with a certain parcel of pasture containing in length 8 perches & in width at one head 4 perches & at the other head 2 perches, to hold to himself & his issue, yearly at the usual terms, this being the 2nd year. And for 18d. from the new rent of the same John for 1 acre of demesne land lying in 'le Worthene', to hold to himself & his heirs, saving the right of anyone, yearly at the same terms, this being the 2nd year. And for 3d. from the new rent of Richard Skileman for 1 piece of land lying at the head of his messuage in the field called 'Newefeld'', containing in length 5 perches & in width at one head 18 feet & at the other head 8 feet, together with entry and exit to carry & to drive from the town of 'Thaxstede' by the bridge called 'Shepecotebregge' unto his messuage, to hold to himself & his, at the term of [*Saint*] Michael, this being the 2nd year.

Sum 19li. 19s. 10½d. — it is tested.

Unfixed rents

And for 16d. from 4 geese of the rents of the term of [*Saint*] Michael sold at the value per head, **4d.** And for [6s. 9d. *struck through,* 9s. *interlined*] from 27 capons of the rents at the term of the Nativity of the lord sold at the value per head [3d. *struck through,* 4d. *interlined in a different hand*]. And for 4d. from 2 hens of the rents at the term of the Nativity of the Lord sold at the value per head, **2d.** And for 8¼d. from 165 eggs of the rents at the term of Easter sold at the value per hundred, **5d.** And for 10½d. from 7 [barbed *interlined*] arrows of the rents at the term of Easter, at the value of each, **1½d.** And for 7s. from 7 plough-shares of the rents at the term of Saint Botolph sold at the value of each, **12d.** And for 3d. from 1 pound of cumin from the rents at the term of Easter sold.

Sum 19s. 5¾d. — it is tested.

Rents of assize of the borough, tolls of the market & fairs

And for 46s. 7½d. from the rents of the borough at the term of Easter. And for 46s. 7½d. from the rents there at the term of Saint Michael. And for 4s. 4d. from the farm of the stalls in the market at the terms of Easter & Saint Michael. And for 5s. from the tolls of the market at the same terms. And for 6d. from the new rent of Thomas Lightfot for 1 piece of land at the eastern head of the grange of the manor. And for 16d. from the new rent of William atte Hyde for 1 piece of land of the lord's garden next his messuage. And for 4d. from the new rent of Walter Walkelyn opposite his tenement at the same terms. And for 1d. from the new rent of Walter Camberleyn for 1 purpresture next his house. And for 2d. from the new rent of John Frend' for 1 piece in the enclosure of the manor between the lord's granary & his house at the same terms. And for ½d. from the new rent of John de la Vyle for 1 piece of land in 'Bolefordegardyn' at the same terms. And for 4d. from the new rent of William Cotiller' for 1 piece of land within the manor next the granary on the eastern part. And for 4d. from the new rent of Robert Cretyng' for 1 piece of land there at the same terms. And for ¼d. from the new rent of John Latonner' for a certain footway next his garden going through a postern-gate as far as 'Newefeld'', at the term of Saint Michael. And for 1d. from the new rent of John Frend' for 1 piece of curtilage between the granary & the room of the steward, containing 40 feet in length & 8 feet in width, at the terms of Easter & Saint Michael. And for 1½d. from the new rent of William Lyon for 2 purprestures in the market-place next the eastern stile of the churchyard thus demised to him, at the same [terms *interlined in a different hand*]. And for 1d. from the new rent of Walter Camberlayn for 1 piece of land next his house at the same terms. And for 4d. from William atte Grene for 2 purprestures demised to him at the will of the lord in the borough, next his house, as the metes and bounds are divided, at the terms aforesaid. And for 6d. from the new rent of Walter Ailwyne for 1 piece between his messuage & the great ditch leading into 'Asshfeld'' towards the bridge in the borough of the town aforesaid, as the metes are divided, thus demised to him, at the terms aforesaid. And for 4s. from Thomas Lightfot for 1 parcel of the lord's garden below his messuage thus demised to him, at the terms aforesaid. And for 6d. from Robert

Cretyng' for 1 piece of vacant land on the south side of his dwelling thus demised at the will of the lord, at the terms aforesaid. And for 1d. from Richard Wolmar' for 1 piece of land from the soil of the manor in the high street in 'Thaxstede', thus demised at the will of the lord, at the terms aforesaid. And for ½d. from Roger atte Welde for 1 piece taken in the high street, to hold at the will of the lord, at the terms aforesaid. And for 1d. from William Locsmyth' for 1 piece of land from the soil of the manor in the high street, at the will of the lord, at the terms aforesaid. And for 2d. from the new rent of Walter Walkelyn for 1 purpresture containing in length 28 feet & in width 12 feet, against the messuage sometime of Richard Hirde, at the terms aforesaid. And for 1d. from the new rent of Thomas Broxheued' for 1 purpresture in the high street, at the term of Saint Michael. And for 1d. from the new rent of Walter Russhedale for 1 purpresture in 'Middelrowe', containing in length 30 feet & in width at one head 1 foot & at the other head ½ foot, to hold to himself & his issue (*sequele*), yearly at the 2 terms, this being the 11th year. And for 2d. from Richard Broxheued' for 1 piece of land containing in length 50 feet & in width 3 feet, lying in Great 'Asshefeld'', with entry & exit in the field aforesaid through 1 postern gate, to hold to himself & his issue by the rod, yearly at the said terms, this being the 11th year. And for 1d. from the new rent of Thomas Huberd' for 1 purpresture in 'Middelrowe', containing in length 16 feet & in width 7 feet, to hold to himself & his issue by the rod, yearly at the said 2 terms, this being the 11th year. And for 4d. from the new rent of Walter son of John Clerk' for 1 purpresture there in length 24 feet & in width 12 feet, to hold to himself & his issue, yearly at the said 2 terms, this being the 11th year. And for 4d. from the new rent of John Auenant for 1 purpresture there in length 34 feet & in width at one head 12 feet & at the other head 6 feet, to hold to himself & his issue by the rod, yearly at the said 2 terms, this being the 11th year. And for 1d. from the new rent of Thomas Boltere for 1 gate with exit outside his close in the field of 'Newefeld'' through[1] 1 postern-gate, to hold to himself & his issue by the rod, yearly at the said 2 terms, this being the 11th year. And for 2d. from the new rent of John Kent for 1 purpresture next his tenement in which there is a water course, containing in length 96 feet & in width 24 feet, to hold to himself & his heirs, yearly at the terms of Easter & Saint Michael equally, this being the 10th year. And for ½d. from the new rent of John Monde for 1 purpresture in which there is a water course next his tenement, in length 60 feet & in width at one head 29 feet & at the other head 27 feet, to hold to himself & his heirs by the rod, yearly at the terms aforesaid, this being the 10th year. And for ½d. from the new rent of John Kent for 1 purpresture between the tenement of Henry de Yerdelee & the bridge called 'Chaloneresbrigge', containing in length 20 feet & in width 10 feet, to hold to himself & his heirs by the rod, yearly at the said 2 terms, this being the 9th year. And for 2d. from the new rent of Thomas Boltere for having entry & exit with horses & carts from the tenement of the said Thomas into the field of 'Newefeld'' over the soil of the lord in the town of 'Thaxstede' beyond the bridge of 'Shepecotebregge', & from the tenement of the said Thomas to a certain piece of his land lying in the said field of 'Newefeld'' as often & whenever he shall require, to hold to himself & his heirs, yearly at the said 2 terms, this being the 9th year. And for 1d. from the new rent of Walter Russhedale for having a certain exit through 1 postern-gate from his tenement into the field of 'Shepecotefeld'', to hold to himself & his heirs by the rod, yearly at the said 2 terms, this being the 7th year. And for 2d. from the new rent of Thomas Boltere for having exit through 1 postern-gate from his tenement into the lord's field in length 50 feet & width 24 feet, to hold to himself & his heirs, yearly at the said terms, this being the 5th year. And for 1d. from the new rent of Walter Clerk' for having exit outside his tenement through 1 postern-gate, to hold to himself & his heirs, yearly at the said 2 terms, this being the 5th year. And for 3d. from the new rent of John Boyton', the younger, for 1 piece of land in 'Newefeld'' next the tenement of the said John, containing in length 5 perches & in width at one head 1½ perches & at the other head 1 perch, to hold to himself & his heirs with freedom of entry & exit through 1 postern-gate by the rod, saving the right of anyone, yearly at the said terms, this being the 4th year. And for 2d. from the new rent of Thomas Mannyng' for 1 piece of land lying in 'Newefeld'' next the tenement

[1] 'pro' written for 'per' in the original.

of the said Thomas, containing in length 3 perches and in width 25 feet, to hold to himself & his heirs by the rod, saving the right of anyone, yearly at the said terms, this being the 4th year. And for 18d. from the new rent of William Pamphilon' for 1 piece of curtilage containing in length 6 perches & 3 parts of 1 perch and in width 1½ perches, lying in 'Bernewik'', with liberty of entry & exit outside his own tenement, to hold to himself & his heirs, yearly at the said terms, this being the 4th year. And for 2d. from the [increase *struck through*, new *interlined*] rent of Thomas May for 1 piece of land in 'Newefeld'' next his own tenement, containing in length 4 perches & in width at one head 25 feet and at the other head 1 perch, to hold to himself & his heirs, yearly at the said terms, this being the 4th year. And for 2d. from the new rent of William Botelmakere for 1 piece of land containing in length 60 feet and in width 30 feet lying next 'Bulefordegardyn', to hold to himself & his heirs, yearly at the said terms, this being the 4th year. And for 4d. from the new rent of Janyn Sawyere for 1 piece of land lying between the lord's garden on the one part & the highway on the other, containing in length 64 feet and in width 30 feet, to hold to himself & his heirs by the rod, saving the right of anyone, yearly at the said terms, this being the 4th year. And for 1d. from the new rent of Walter Fot for 1 purpresture containing in length 14 feet [&] in width 3 feet, lying next his tenement, to hold to himself & his heirs, yearly at the said terms, this being the 4th year. And for 4d. from the new rent of Andrew Neel for 1 purpresture of land lying next 'Bolefordegardyn', containing in length 64 feet & in width 47 feet, to hold to himself & his heirs, yearly, this being the 3rd year, saving the right of anyone, at the said terms. And for 2d. from the new rent of William Camberleyn for 1 purpresture containing in length 46 feet & in width 2 feet next his tenement, to hold to himself & his heirs by the rod at the will of the lord, yearly at the terms of Easter & Saint Michael, this being the 2nd year. And for 3d. from the new rent of John Munde for ½ rood of land lying in 'Newefeld'', to hold to himself & his issue yearly at the usual terms, this being the 2nd year. And for 1d. from the new rent of Andrew Sibbe for 1 purpresture lying in 'le Middelrowe' next his messuage on the south part, containing in length 26 feet & in width at one head 3½ feet & at the other head nothing, to hold to himself & his issue, yearly at the usual terms, this being the 2nd year. And for 1d. from the new rent of John Sibily for 1 purpresture next his houses, in width 1½ feet & length 12 feet, to hold to himself & his, yearly at the said terms, this being the 2nd year.

Sum 117s. 2¾d. — it is tested.

Farms of land

And for 20s. from the farm of 1 virgate of land, sometime of John Punt & Hugh Punt, thus demised to John Godard', yearly at the 4 terms. And for 20s. from the farm of 40 acres of land, sometime 'Doketteslond'', thus demised to John Benge for a term of 12 years, this being the 2nd year, yearly at the said 4 terms. And for 12s. from the farm of 16 acres of land & 1 acre of meadow, sometime of Pamphilon', thus demised to Henry Monde, at the same terms. And for 6s. 10d. from the farm of 20½ acres of demesne land in 'Northfeld'' thus demised to John Benge, at the same terms. And for 5s. from Master Thomas Vfforde, vicar there, for the farm of 1 croft, sometime of Nicholas atte Hyde, yearly, thus demised to the same at the will of the lord, at the said terms. And for 2s. 2d. from the new farm of Thomas Woubourne for 1 croft of land & 1 piece of curtilage called 'Rollecoescroft' thus demised to the same for the term of his life, yearly at the said terms. And for 7s. 6d. from John Clerk' for the farm of 13 acres 3 roods of demesne land in 'Boxstede' with 1 piece of pasture called 'Alsichewelle' thus demised to the same, yearly at the same terms. And for 2s. 8d. from the farm of 5 acres of demesne land there thus demised to John Smyth' at the will of the lord, yearly at the said terms. And for 4s. from the farm of 5 roods of meadow in 'Northmad'' thus demised to John Benge, at the same terms. And for 14s. from John Terry from the farm of ½ virgate of land called 'Cokattes', sometime of Richard Herberd', thus demised to the same & his heirs, saving the right of anyone, this being the fourth year, as appears in the court held there the 7th day of the month of October in the 1st year. And for 20s. from John Crakeman for the farm of ½ virgate of land called 'Shymmyngeslond'' thus demised to the same for a term of 12 years, this being the 2nd year. And for 8s. from John Cartere for the farm of the tenement formerly of John Peyt, akerman, thus demised to the same this year [and is usually leased for **12s.** *interlined*]. And for 3s. from John Heldere for the farm of the tenement called 'Bretoneslond'', of coterell tenure, thus demised to the same this year. For **15d.** for 1 croft of land, sometime of John Baillie, next the mill, nothing here, because it is rented to John Sale, as appears above, paid within. And for 3s. from John Hastere [*recte,* Haftere] for the farm of 6 acres of demesne land in — 'Boxstede', formerly in the hands of William Fromond', thus demised to the same this year. And for 11s. from John Godard' for the farm of ½ virgate of land, sometime of Amice Alein, this year. And for 12s. from the same John for the farm of ½ virgate of land, sometime of William Marchal, this year. And for 18s. from Robert Trubbok' for the farm of ½ virgate of land. sometime of Thomas Waltham, formerly of Walter Scamp', this year. And for 14s. from from John Wrighte for the farm of ½ virgate of land, sometime of John Alein, this year. And for 8s. from John Abraham for the farm of 1 akerman's land, sometime of John Cook', this year. And for 8s. from John son of Thomas Godard' for the farm of 1 akerman's land, sometime of John Grene, thus demised to the same this year. For **3s.** from John Monde for the farm of 1 coterell's bond land sometime of William Heldere, nothing because for works & other services. And for 2s. from John son of Adam Herry for the farm of 1 cottage with a certain curtilage, sometime of Richard Daubere, in the hands of the lord by the name of escheat, demised for a term of 20 years, this being the 11th year, yearly at the 4 terms. And for 5s. from John Abraham for the farm of ½ akerman's land, formerly of Matilda Haftere, containing 5 acres, thus demised to the same for the term of 12 years, this being the 2nd year, yearly at the said terms. And for 4s. from William Tyle for 1 coterell's land called 'Rammes', formerly in the hands of Thomas Fisshere, thus demised to the same this year, at the said terms. For **23s. 6d.** from John Yerdele for the farm of 1 piece of land containing 159 acres of the lord's demesne in 'Northfeld'', nothing here, because he answers for 24s. among the farms of demesne land, as in the schedule hereto annexed. And for 3s. 4d. from John son of Adam Harry for the farm of 1 croft of land called 'Brightmannescrot' [*sic*], of coterell tenure, to hold to himself at the will of the lord, yearly at the 4 terms, this being the 2nd year. And for 3s. 6d. from John Stace for the farm of 1 tenement, formerly of Simon Smyth', of coterell tenure, thus demised to the same for a term of 12 years, this being the 2nd year, yearly at the said terms.

Sum 10li. 17s. — it is tested.

New farms of the issue of the demesne

And for [41li. 8s. received *inserted in a different hand*] from the farm of demesne lands, meadows & pastures demised to divers men, as appears by the parcels annexed hereto.

Sum 41li. 8s. — it is tested.

Issue of the manor

And for 40s. from 1500 faggots made in the little park & 'Southfrith'' sold this year, at the value **per thousand, 26s. 8d.** [1]And for 30s. from 1500 faggots made in 'Oldefrith'' this year, at the value **per hundred, 2s.** And for 13s. 4d. from the haymaking (*relucro*) of 32 acres of meadow in 'Parkmed'' & 4 acres in 'Pamphilonnesmede' thus sold this year. And the haymaking from 'Parkmed'' was accustomed to be sold for **20s.** & 'Pamphilonnesmed'' for **18d.**

Sum 4li. 3s. 4d. — it is tested.

Agistment of the parks

For the agistment of divers beasts sent out into 'Southfrith'' nothing this year, on account of the multitude of beasts of the chase there, by witness of the Receiver of the account. And for 10s. 6d. from the agistment of divers beasts sent out into the little park there, as appears by the parcels examined upon the account.

Sum 10s. 6d. — it is tested.

[1] Remainder of section in a different hand.

Sale of pasture

From the sale of pasture nothing here, because it is contained among the items of the new farms of demesne as in the schedule annexed hereto. And for 44s. from the hay of 12 acres 3½ roods of meadow sold to divers men, that is to say, John Hert **20s.**, John Camberleyn **12s.**, John Serle **8s.**, John Wolpet **4s.**

Sum 44s. — it is tested.

Sale of works

And[1] for 2s. 9¾d. from the making of 11 quarters 2 bushels of malt barley from the issues of the customary tenants sold, per quarter, **3d.** And 30s. from 90 ploughings from the issues of the same sold at the value per ploughing, **4d.** And for 38s. 5½d. from 923 winter works from the issues of the same sold at the value per work, **½d.** And for 14s. 1½d. from 169½ summer works from the issues of the same sold at the value per work, **1d.** And for 40s. 4d. from 484 autumn works from the issues of the same sold at the value per work, **1d.**

Sum 6li. 5s. 8¾d. — it is tested.

Sale of corn

And for 28s. 4d. received from 5 quarters of wheat from the farm of the mills there, whereof **2 quarters 4 bushels** at the value per quarter, **5s. 4d.**, & **2 quarters 4 bushels** at the value per quarter, **6s.** And for 24s. — from 4 quarters of wheat from the farm of the same sold at the value per quarter, **6s.** And for 15s. from 5 quarters of multure from the farm of the said mills sold at the value per quarter, **3s.** And for 13s. 4d. from 4 quarters of multure from the farm of the same afterwards sold at the value per quarter, **3s. 4d.**

Sum 4li. 8d. — it is tested.

Perquisites of the courts

And for [14li. 2s. 7d. *inserted in a different hand*] from the perquisites of 13 courts held there this year with 1 leet.

Sum 14li. 2s. 7d. — it is tested.

External receipts

[Nothing this year, *inserted in a different hand*].

Sales on the account

[And for 13s. 8d. from divers things sold on the account as without, *inserted in a different hand*].

Sum 13s. 8d. — it is tested.

Sum total of receipts with arrears, 184li. 7s. 9½d. — it is tested.

Allowances & deductions of rent

Thereof he reckons in deduction of the rent of the tenement, sometime Pamphilons, because in the hands of the lord & at farm above, yearly at the 4 terms, 4s. 4d. And in deduction of the rent of 1 croft, sometime of Nicholas atte Hyde, in the hands of the lord, yearly, 3s. And in deduction of the rent of 1 piece, sometime of William Dauy & Robert Carpenter', in the hands of the lord, & there is the ditch (*fouea*) for enclosing the lord's garden & 'Bulfordegardyn' unto the piece sometime of Pykel, yearly at the terms of Easter & Saint Michael, 16½d. And in deduction of the rent of 1 piece of Osebert Anable & Geoffrey Miller (*Molendinar'*), lying in the highway towards 'Berdefeld'', in the hands of the lord & lying vacant, at the same terms, 6d. [of the allowance of the borough *interlined*]. And in deduction of the rent [of 1 piece *interlined*] sometime of Geoffrey Ilger', Robert Cappe & Philip Smith (*Fabri*), because in the hands of the lord, lying vacant at the same terms, 10d. [of the allowance of the borough *interlined*]. And in deduction of the rent of 1 stall, sometime of Thomas Montioye, in the hands of the lord, lying vacant in the Borough, at the same [terms], 2d. [allowance of the borough *interlined*]. And in deduction of the rent of 1 croft of land containing 1½ acres,

[1] Whole of this section in a different hand.

sometime of John Baillie, in the hands of the lord & at farm above, yearly at the 4 terms, 2s. 2d. And in deduction of the rent of 1 stall, sometime of Andrew Campyon', of 1 stall, sometime of William atte Noke, & William Homan, of 1 stall, sometime of Henry Hendys, of 1 stall, sometime of Adam Seynt Albons & Nicholas atte Hyde, of 1 stall, sometime of Richard Horel, of 1 stall, sometime of William atte Hel, of 1 stall, sometime of Jane de Berdefeld' & William Tannere, of 3 stalls of John Pulcoo, of 1 stall, sometime of Edmund Danyel, of 1 stall, sometime of Richard Arnold' & Roger Huberd', of 1 stall, sometime of John Puntfreys, of 1 stall, sometime of John Hydeman & William son of John Shethere, & of 1 stall, sometime of John Spayne & Thomas Flatbacon', in the hands of the lord by default of the tenants during the same time, 2s. 6d., that is to say, for each stall, **2d.** [allowance of the borough *interlined*]. And in deduction of the rent of 1 cottage with curtilage, sometime of Richard Daubere, in the hands of the lord by name of escheat & at farm above to John son of Adam Harry, yearly, 4d. And in deduction of the rent of 1 coterell's land, sometime 'Rammes', in the hands of the lord, this being the 10th year, & at farm to William Tyle as above, yearly, 12d. And in deduction of the rent of 1 croft of land with 1 curtilage, sometime Rullecoes, because in the hands of the lord & at farm above to Thomas Woubourne, yearly, 4d. this being the 10th year. [And in deduction of the external rents above charged, because it is unknown when they ought to be levied, as had been examined throughout the rents of every tenant by Thomas de Hildeburghe, whereof the particulars named are entered in a certain new rental, yearly, 24s. 11½d. *struck through,* until it is better ascertained *interlined*].

Sum 16s. 6½d. — it is tested.

Expenses of necessaries

And in making 1 'bay' in 'le Parkmed'', in all, 6s. 8d. And in payment of 2 sawyers for 2 days sawing 'rayles & plankes' for the same, 20d., taking between themselves daily **10d.** And in the contract of John Proude & John Parleben, carpenters, to make anew 1 footbridge called 'Serlesbregge', in all, 9s. And in payment of 2 sawyers for 5 days sawing 'plankes & railes' for the said bridge, 4s. 2d., taking daily **10d.** And in 1 cart hired for 1 day to carry timber to the said 'bay' & bridge, 16d. And in the cart hired for 2 days to carry sand & clay to the said bridge, 2s. And in payment of 3 men for 4 days filling the said cart & ramming the clay & sand around the aforesaid bridge 3s., to each daily [**4d.** *struck through,* 3d. *interlined*]. And in payment of John Serunt, mason, for 10 days footing anew the bridge called 'Chalonneresbregg'' & newly making a stone wall on either side of the ditch of the said bridge [5s. *struck through,* 4s. 2d. *interlined*], per day [**6d.** *struck through,* 5d. *interlined*]. And in payment of 2 men for the same earning during the same term, 5s., taking between them daily **6d.** And in payment of 1 man for 10 days digging & collecting stones for the aforesaid work, 2s. 6d., per day, **3d.** And in 1 cart hired for 2 days to carry the said stones unto the said bridge, 2s. And in payment of 1 man driving & filling the said cart for the same, 6d. And in 9 quarters of burnt lime bought for the aforesaid work on the bridge 12s., at the value per quarter, **16d.** And in 1 cart hired for carrying the said lime at Walden, 4s. And in 1 cart hired for 1 day to carry sand to the same work, 12d. And in payment of 1 man digging the said sand, 3d. And in payment of 1 man for 1 day felling timber in the park there for the aforesaid bridge, 3d. And in payment of William Wrighte for 10 days newly making & constructing the said bridge, 3s. 4d., taking per day **4d.** And in payment of 2 sawyers for 4 days sawing 'plankes & railles' for the said bridge, 3s. 4d. And in 1 cart hired to carry the said timber unto the said bridge, 16d. And in the expenses of divers men helping to carry the said timber into the said cart, 4d. And in 1 cart hired for 2 days carrying sand & putting amid the said work stone & earth, 2s. And in payment of 1 man for 2 days filling the said cart with the said sand, 6d. And in scouring 65 perches of ditch in 'Parkmad'' to make free the water-course from the said park 10s. 10d., per perch, **2d.** And to the same in the value of 1 bushell of wheat by custom, 9d. [4li. 23d. up to here *added in margin in a different hand*]. [1]And in payment of 2 masons for 2 days repairing the said stone wall thus

[1] Remainder of section in a different hand.

emplaced [*which was*] carried away and destroyed by the flood of water arriving in the month of May, 20d., to either daily [**6d.** *struck through,* 5d. *interlined*]. And in payment to 2 like [*masons*] earning during the same time, 12d., to either daily, **3d.** And in 1 quarter 4 bushels of burnt lime bought for the same work, 2s., at the value per quarter, **16d.** And in the carriage of the same lime from Walden' unto here, 9d. And in payment of 1 man for 2 days collecting stones for the same work, 6d. And in the carriage of sand for the same work, 4d. [Cost of the houses as within *added in margin in a different hand*].

Sum — 4li. 8s. [6d. *struck through,* 2d. *interlined*] — it is tested.

Cost of the mills

And in 2 rods bought for the sails of the mill of 'Cherchemelle', 13s. 4d. And in 1 cart hired for 1 day for carrying the said rods from 'Donmowe', 16d. And in the contract of John Blundel, carpenter, to make anew the said sails & repair the structure of the house of the said mill destroyed & thrown down by the tempest of wind, & to mend divers faults of the said mill, of a carpentry nature, in all, 13s. 4d. And in the expenses of divers men helping in boon service to raise & implace the new work, 12d. And in iron nails bought for the said work, 10d. [1]And in divers costs made & pledged about the repair of the mills of 'Northmulle' & 'Cherchemulle' at the end of the year, as appears by the parcels hereto annexed, 56s. 10d.

Sum — 4li. 6s. 8d. — it is tested.

Costs of the houses

And[1] in divers costs made about the repair of the houses of the manor at the end of the year, as appears by the parcels hereto annexed, 12s.

Sum — 12s. — it is tested.

Costs of the park

And in making anew 36 perches of fencing around the [little *interlined*] park at 'les Busshes', 9s., per perch, **3d.** And in 20 perches of fencing repaired, 20d. And in 1 cart hired for 1 day to carry the fencing & timber to the said enclosure 16d. And in payment of 2 men for 2 days mending the hedges of the park between 'les Hulles' & the road of the park, 12d., to either daily, **3d.** And in making 200 perches of new hedge around the great park, 33s. 4d., per perch, **2d.** [in the value of 4 winter-works *interlined*]. And in 60 perches of new hedge there made afterwards, 15s., per perch, **3d.** [1]And in divers costs made about the repair of the lodge & the enclosure of the park there at the end of the year, as appears by the parcels hereto annexed, 8s. 5d.

Sum — 69s. 9d. — it is tested.

Mowing of the meadows

In mowing 18 acres 2½ roods of meadow, nothing here because by the works of the customary tenants as without. In tedding the cut grass thereof, nothing here for the reason aforesaid. And in the custom of the customary tenants after mowing the meadows for their ram, 12d. In making the hay of the same, nothing here, because by the works without. And in the custom of 2 carts of the customary tenants carrying the hay of the lord from the meadows into the grange for 1 day, 6d., to either cart by custom **3d.** [1]And in turning, gathering and making the hay of 4 acres of meadow in 'Pamphilonesmed'' by men hired for the same, 16d.

Sum — 2s. 10d. — it is tested.

Wages & payments

And in payment of John Godard', bailiff there, yearly, 60s. 8d., taking per day **2d.** And in the payment and clothes of the same during the same time, because he has taken nothing from the livery of the lord, 16s. 8d. And in the wages of Walter Clerk', collector of the rents & of the court of the borough, this year, 6s. 8d.

Sum — 4li. 4s. — it is tested.

[1] Remainder of section in a different hand.

Annuities

And paid to Hugh Huse for a certain annuity granted to him by the lord for the term of the life of the same Hugh, granted to be received of this manor [1]yearly at the terms of Easter & [Saint] Michael equally by charter of the same lord according to the warrant annexed to the account of the 6th year preceding, that is to say, for the terms of [*Saint*] Michael & Easter in the 4th year 40s., by 1 acquittance on the account paid. And in the annuity of the same at the term of [*Saint*] Michael at the end of this year by the hands of Walter Roc, 20s., by 1 acquittance on the account paid. And in the annuity of **100s.** granted by the lord to John Brag' for the term of his life, to be received of this manor at the said terms equally, nothing here because on the account of the Receiver of Clare on this occasion.

Sum — 60s. — it is tested.

Payment of the farm

And paid to Master Richard le Scrop' for the farm of the 4th part of the manor appertaining to Lord Tibbetot this year at the terms of Easter & Saint Michael, at the will of the lord to be continued, that is to say, for the term of Easter this year, 13li. 6s. 8d., by 1 acquittance on the account paid. [Henceforth the acquittance shall be had under the seal of the said Richard *added in margin in a different hand*].

Sum — 13li. 6s. 8d. — it is tested.

External expenses

[And in the expenses of 1 man with 1 horse carrying 1 doe to London to Lord John Louell', in escheat, 20d. *struck through*]. And in the expenses of Thomas de Hidelburghe, the Constable, & others being here for taking the view of the account there made & others superintending things, 3s. 10d.

Sum — 3s. 10d. — it is tested.

Payment of money received

And paid to William Aillemer', Receiver of Clare, by the hand of the said accountant by 2 tallies, 63li., whereof the first contains **40li.** & the second **23li.**

Sum 63li.

Sum of all the allowances & payments — 97li. 10s. 5½d. And owes — 86li. 17s. 4d. From which is allowed to the same accountant, 14s. — from divers things overcharged & disallowed in this account. And thus up to here he owes 86li. 3s. 4d. which are charged in the next account for which he answers there. And thus he is quit here.

Whereof are respited 13li. [14]s.[2] 6½d. from the deduction of rents disallowed this year & 10 years previously elapsed, that is to say, **24s. 11½d.** [yearly],[2] until the better examination of the Rental, whereof from the charge of John Neel abovesaid **112s. 3¾d.** And [there is respited][2] 16s. from the deduction of the rent of 3 capons & 1 ploughshare accounted for [*two words illegible*] disallowed this year & 7 years previously elapsed, that is to say, **12d.** yearly for the said ploughshare & **12d.** for [the said 3 capons][2].

Whereof of the charge [of the said John Neel],[2] **10s.** Total respited **14li. 10s. 6[½]d.**[2] [And he owes][2] clear — 7li. 1[2s.][2] 9½d.

Whereof upon

John Neel, formerly bailiff — 14li. 14s. [*torn away*]. John Godard, bailiff, the accountant — 56li. 18s. [*torn away*] of the remainder **23li. 11s. 5½d.** of the arrears of Walter Godar[d][2] [*torn away*] charged on the said John Godard in the preceding account because [*torn away*] who [*one word illegible*] thence to be paid in the year next to come [*torn away*] out of consideration of Lord Peter de la Mare and others of the council [*torn away*] common 10li. 6s. 11½d. Thence is assigned [*torn away*] [*two lines partly torn away, partly illegible*].

[1] Remainder of membrane in a different hand.
[2] Torn away, figures and words supplied.

[*dorse*]

Wheat

The same answers for 6 quarters of wheat from the farm of the mill of 'Cherchemelne' thus demised this year by view of the Constable of Clare, except the multure within. And for [3 quarters *struck through*, 4 quarters *interlined*] from the farm of the mill of 'Northmelne' thus demised by the same during the time aforesaid. [And not more, because **1 quarter** from the farm of the same is withdrawn since the said mill has stood unemployed through lack of repair between the feast of the Nativity of Saint John the Baptist & the feast of [*Saint*] Michael, that is to say, for 1 quarter of the year *struck through*].

Sum — [9 quarters *struck through,* 10 quarters *interlined*]. Whereof in selling as within 9 quarters.

And in selling on the account 1 quarter for 5s. 4d. — And balances.

Multure of the mill

And for 6 quarters from the farm of the mill of 'Cherchemelne' [thus *interlined*] demised this year by view of the said Constable. And for [3 quarters *struck through,* 4 quarters *interlined*] from the farm of the mill of 'Northmelne' thus demised by the same during the time aforesaid. [And no more, because **1 quarter** is withdrawn for the latter quarter of the year for the reason as above under the heading of Wheat *struck through*].

Sum [9 quarters *struck through,* 10 quarters *interlined*]. [Sold as within — And balances *struck through*].

Thence in selling as within 9 quarters. And in selling on the account 1 quarter for 3s.

Sum as above — And balances.

Geese

And for 4 from the rents there yearly at the term of Saint Michael.

Sum — 4 — And sold as within — And balances.

Capons

And for 26 from the rents of the tenants there at the term of the Nativity of the Lord. And for 1 capon from William Alman for licence to use the craft of tanner, at the said term. And for 1 capon from the rent of Richard Latonner at the same term. And for 1 from the chevage of William Stephene, bondman of the lord, at the same term. And for 1 capon from Thomas Hierde for licence to use the craft of tanner and to remain outside the borough, at the same term.

Sum — 30

[Whereof in exoneration of the rents because the bailiff does not know when they ought to be levied or who is held to pay, as was examined throughout particular rents by Thomas de Hildeburgh' in the month of June in the 9th year preceding, 3 *struck through*]. And in selling as within 27. And in selling on the account 3 [*for*] 3d.

Sum as above — And balances.

Hens

And for 2 from the rents there at the Nativity of the Lord — Sum, 2. And sold as within — And balances.

Eggs

And for 285 eggs from the customary rents at the term of Easter — Sum — 285 eggs. For those in deduction of the rents of 4 virgates of land, whereof 1 virgate, formerly of John Punt, 1 virgate, formerly of Richard Herberd' & William Shymmyng', 1 virgate of land, sometime of William Maschal & Amice Aleyn, $\frac{1}{2}$ virgate of land, sometime of Walter Skamp' & $\frac{1}{2}$ virgate of land, sometime of John Alein, because in the hands of the lord & at farm as within — 120 eggs, that is to say, for each virgate, **30 eggs.** And in selling as within 165 eggs.

Sum as above — And balances.

Arrows

And for 7 from the rents there yearly at the term of Easter — Sum — 7 — And sold as within — And balances.

Ploughshares

And for 8 from the rents there yearly at the term of Saint Botolph.

Sum — 8

[Whereof in exoneration of the rents because he does not know when they ought to be levied or who is held to pay, as was examined by the aforesaid Thomas in the month of June in the 9th year preceding, 1 *struck through*]. And in selling as within 7. And in selling on the account 1 [*for*] 12d.

Sum as above — And balances.

Cumin

And for 1 pound of cumin from the rents there at the term of Easter — Sum, 1 pound — And sold as within — And balances.

Garden

For the produce of the garden, nothing here because within at farm.

Account of Works

Making of malt

And for the making of 23 quarters 2 bushels of barley into malt arising from the issue of $7\frac{3}{4}$ virgates of land at the feast of the Nativity of the Lord, whereof each virgater will make 3 quarters of [barley *interlined*] into malt or will give for the making of each quarter **3d.** by custom. Sum of the making — 23 quarters 2 bushels —

Thence in deduction of the 4 virgates of land above said, because in the hands of the lord & at farm as within, the making of 12 quarters of barley into malt. And in selling as within the making of 11 quarters 2 bushels of malt.

Sum as above — And balances.

Customary ploughing, value of the ploughing of each acre **4d.**

And for the ploughing of 186 acres of land arising from $7\frac{3}{4}$ virgates of land at the seasons of winter, Lent and fallow, whereof each virgater will plough at each season 8 acres of land.

Sum of the ploughing — 186 acres.

Whereof in deduction of the ploughing of the aforesaid 4 virgates for the reason abovesaid, the ploughing of 96 acres. And in selling as within the ploughing of 90 acres.

Sum as above — And balances.

Winter works, value of the work **$\frac{1}{2}$d.**

And for $1472\frac{1}{2}$ works arising by custom from the customary tenants holding among themselves $7\frac{3}{4}$ virgates of land between the feast of [*Saint*] Michael & the feast of the Nativity of Saint John the Baptist during 38 weeks for certain, whereof each virgate of land will do each week during the same time **5 works**, that is to say, during Monday, Tuesday, Wednesday, Thursday & Friday, unless feast days shall fall on those days. And thus from each virgate **190 works.** And for 684 works arising from 9 akermen during the same time, whereof each holds 10 acres of land & does each week **2 works.** And thus from each of them **76 works.** And for 418 works arising from 11 coterells during the same time, whereof each does each week **1 work**. And thus from each of them **38 works.**

Sum — $2574\frac{1}{4}$ works.

Whereof in deduction of the works of the 4 virgates of land aforesaid for the reason abovesaid, 760 works. And in allowance of the works of the aforesaid $3\frac{3}{4}$ virgates of land, for the ploughing of 90 acres of land as above at the 3 seasons by the custom called 'Gauelerthe', 225 works, that is to say, for the ploughing of each acre **$2\frac{1}{2}$ works**. And in allowance of the works of the same for 4 feast weeks during the same time, that is to say, the fortnight of the Nativity of the Lord, the weeks of Easter & Pentecost, 75 works. And in allowance of the works of the same for 18 feast days falling during their working days within the said time, that is to say, Saint Luke the

Evangelist on Thursday, All Saints on Thursday, All Souls on Friday, Saint Edward the King on Tuesday, Saint Clement the Pope of Friday, Saint Andrew the Apostle on Friday, Saint Nicholas on Thursday, Saint Thomas the Apostle on Friday, the Conversion of Saint Paul on Friday, the Cathedra of Saint Peter on Friday, Saint Gregory the Pope on Tuesday, the Annunciation of the Blessed Mary on Monday, Saint Mark the Evangelist on Thursday, the Apostles Philip & James on Wednesday, the Invention of the [*Holy*] Cross on Friday, the Ascension of the Lord on Thursday, Saint Barnabas the Apostle on Tuesday, Corpus Christi on Thursday, 67½ works, that is to say, for each virgate each day, **1 work**. And in deduction of the works of 3½ akermen, that is to say, 1 John Peyt, 1 John Cook', 1 John Grene & ½ Matilda Haftere, because in the hand of the lord & at farm as within, 266 works, for each akerman **76 works**. And in deduction of the works of the tenement of John Yonge, ½ akerman, in the hand of the lord by default of the tenant, this being the 5th year, 38 works. And in allowance of the works of 5 akermen working during the 4 weeks abovesaid, 40 works, for each akerman, **8 works**. And in deduction of the works of 1 coterell's [land] called 'Bretonneslond'' because in the hand of the lord & at farm as within, 38 works. And in deduction of the works of 1 coterell's land called 'Rammes', sometime of Matilda Fisshere, because in the hands of the lord & at farm as within to William Tyle, 38 works. And in deduction of the works of 1 coterell's [*land*] called 'Bryght mannescroft' in the hand of the lord, this being the 2nd year, & to farm as within to John son of Adam Harry, 38 works. And in default of the works of the tenement, formerly of Simon Smyth', coterell, in the hand of the lord, this being the 2nd year, & at farm as within to John Stace, 38 works. And in allowance of the works of 7 coterells working during the 4 feast weeks abovesaid by custom, 28 works. [1]In the enclosure of the hedges of the park nothing here [because *interlined*] for money as within. And in selling as within 923 works.

Sum as above — And balances.

Summer works, value of the work **1d.**

And for 418½ summer [works *interlined*] arising by custom from the customary tenants holding among themselves 7¾ virgates of land between the feast of the Nativity of Saint John the Baptist & Lammas Day, during 5 weeks & 2 days for working this year; they (*qui*) will work for each virgate of land weekly **10 works** for the aforesaid 5 days for working, unless a feast day shall fall on those days. And thus for each virgate, **54 works**. And for 99 works arising from the aforesaid 9 akermen during the same time, whereof each [will do *interlined*] weekly **2 works**. And for 55 works arising from 11 coterells during the same time, whereof each will do weekly **1 work**. And for 30 works arising from 6 Cotmen during the same time, whereof each will do weekly 1 work & will not work except, however, in Autumn. And for 1 work arising from Richard Ailmer' for making the lord's hay.

Sum 603½ works — it is tested.

Whereof in deduction of the works of the aforesaid 4 virgates for the reason aforesaid, 216 works. And in allowance of the works of the aforesaid 3¾ virgates of land for 2 feast days falling on their working days within the said time, that is to say, Saint Mary Magdalene on Monday, Saint James the Apostle on Thursday, **15 works**. And in deduction of the works of the aforesaid 3 [½ *interlined*] akermen in the hands of the lord for the reason as above, 38½ works. And in deduction of the works of the tenement of John Yonge, ½ akerman, in the hand of the lord by default of the tenant, this being the 5th year, 5¼ works. And in deduction of the works of [2 *interlined*] coterells abovesaid for the reason aforesaid, 10 works. And in deduction of the works of the aforesaid 2 coterell's [*lands*], whereof 1 is called 'Brightmannescroft' & 1, formerly of Simon Smyth', in the hand of the lord, this being the 2nd year, as above, 10 works. And in allowance of the works of the aforesaid 3¾ virgates of land for mowing 18 acres 2½ roods of meadow in 'Parkmad'' & 'Pamphilonesmad'', 37[¼ *interlined*] works, that is to say, per acre, **2 works**. Nevertheless each virgater will mow **9 acres**, if it shall be needed, by custom. And in allowance of the works of the same for making, collecting and making into cocks the hay of the said meadow with the help of the cotmen as

[1] Remainder of section in a different hand.

within, 30 works, that is to say, from each virgater by custom **8 works.** And in allowance of the works of the aforesaid 5 akermen, 7 coterells & 6 cotmen working to make the said hay & to make [*it*] into cocks by custom, 72 works, for each of them, **4 works.** In[1] allowance [of the works *interlined*] of divers customary tenants for turning, removing & making the hay of 4 acres of meadow in 'Pamphilonesmede', because not of the demesne of the manor, that is to say, from each of them daily **2** works, nothing here because for money as within. And in selling as within 169½ works.

Sum as above — And balances.

Autumn works, value of the work **1d.**

And for 651 works arising by custom from the customary tenants holding among themselves 7¾ virgates of land between Lammas Day & the feast of Saint Michael falling on Sunday this year, that is to say, for 8 weeks & 2 days for working; they (*qui*) will work for each virgate of land weekly **10 works** during the aforesaid 5 working days, unless feast days shall fall on those days. And thus for each virgate, **84 works.** And for 144 works arising from 9 akermen during the same time, whereof each does weekly **2 works.** And for 88 works arising from 11 coterells during the same time, whereof each will do weekly **1 work.** And for 48 works arising from 6 cotmen during the same time, whereof each does weekly **1 work.**

Sum — 931 works.

Whereof in deduction of the works of the aforesaid 4 virgates for the reason aforesaid, 336 works, that is to say, for each virgate, **84 works.** And in allowance of the works of the aforesaid 3¾ virgates of land for 2 feast days falling on their working days during the aforesaid time, that is to say, the Assumption of the Blessed Mary & the Decollation of Saint John the Baptist on Thursday, 15 works. And in default of the works of 4 akermen abovesaid, because in the hand of the lord as above, 64 works. And in default of the works of 4 coterells as above for the reason aforesaid 32 works. [2]And in selling as within 484 works.

Sum as above — And balances.

Meadows

And for 27 acres — of meadow in 'Northmed'', except **1 acre 1 rood** at farm to John Bynge in the account by itself, in 'Parkmed' 32 acres, in 'Pamphilonesmad'' 4 acres, in Brodefan 12 acres, and in Shepecotemad' 21 acres.

Sum 96 acres — it is tested.

[Whereof in the sustenance of 1 horse of the baliff at summer time this year, 1 acre *struck through*]. And there were mown by the customary tenants 18 acres 2½ roods. And in selling as within this year, as appears by a certain schedule annexed hereto, 76 acres 1½ roods. And in selling on the account the grass of 1 acre for 3s. 4d.

Sum as above — And balances.

Hay

And for the hay of 6 acres of meadow of the remainder. And for the hay of 18 acres 2½ roods of meadow from the mowing this year.

Sum of hay 24 acres 2½ roods.

Whereof in [*illegible*] the hay of 1 acre 3 roods. And in the expenses of the horses of the Steward, Constable, Auditors & others of the lord's council, the hay of 4 acres. And in the sustenance of the wild beasts in winter time this year the hay of 2 acres. And in selling as within the hay of 12 acres 3½ roods.

And there remains the hay of 4 acres of meadow.

[1] Remainder of section in a different hand.

[2] Remainder of dorse in a different hand.

ORIGINAL SOURCES CONSULTED

MANORIAL RECORDS

Manor and Borough of Thaxted

Compoti, 1361-2, 1377-8 and 1380-1	E.R.O.,	D/DHu M1
Survey, 1393		D/DHu M58
Court rolls (include Spencers Fee), 1468-1672		D/DHu M1-5
Surveys and Rentals, most of these include the Manors of Horham Hall, Spencers Fee and Coldhams Fee, 1405-07 (Borough only), 1416, 1449 (Spencers Fee only), 1484, 1577, 1593, 1598, 1601, *c.*1605, 1629, 1639, 1646, 1651, 1663, 1675, 1686		D/DHu M18-35
Compoti, 1404, *c.*1467-*c.*1470, 1514		D/DHu M62-63

Manor of Horham Hall

Court rolls, 1394-1672	D/DHu M64-75
Rentals, 1442, 1507	D/DHu M82-83

Manor of Richmonds

Court roll, 1605-1641	D/DHw M2
Do., 1623	D/DBa M8
Rental, 1682	D/DK M149

Manor of Priors Hall

Court roll, 1456-1459, 1494-1501, 1507-1570	D/DMg M121
Rental, 1420	D/DMg M117
Rental, 1646	D/DMg M122

DEEDS AND OTHER COGNATE DOCUMENTS

Horham Hall Estate and the Manor and Borough of Thaxted, 1311-1881	D/DHu T1-28 ; D/DSh T1-9, T36-63
Copy of Charter of Incorporation of the Borough of Thaxted, 1556	D/DHu T29
Legal papers in Cutts *v* Mayor and Bailiffs of Thaxted in the Courts of Wards and Liveries	D/DHu T30
Manor of Richmonds with the Great and Little Parks in Thaxted, 1503-1654	D/DGh T27-32

MAPS

Tithe Map of Thaxted, 1844	D/CT 348
Thaxted Lodge and Richmonds Farm, 1737	D/DHw P5

OTHER RECORDS

Poll Tax Return for Thaxted, 1381	P.R.O.,	E179/107/49

BIBLIOGRAPHY

Primary Printed Sources

Calendars of Close Rolls (Volumes as cited in footnotes to *Introduction*)

Calendars of Inquisitions Post-Mortem (Volumes as cited in footnotes to *Introduction*)

Calendars of Patent Rolls (Volumes as cited in footnotes to *Introduction*)

Secondary Printed Sources

The Complete Peerage (Volumes as cited in footnotes to *Introduction*)

Victoria County History, Essex, Vol. I (1907)

H. S. Bennett, *Life on the English Manor, 1150-1400* (Cambridge, 1938)

J. H. Clapham, *A Concise Economic History of Britain* (Cambridge, 1949)

E. Lamond (ed.) *Walter of Henley's Husbandry, together with an anonymous Husbandry, Seneschaucie, etc.* (Royal Hist. Soc., 1890)

A. Levett, *Black Death on the Estates of the Bishopric of Winchester* (Oxford, 1916)

D. Monteith, *Saffron Walden and its Environs* (unpublished M.A. thesis, University of London, 1958)

P. Morant, *History and Antiquities of Essex* (1768), Vol. II

C. Oman, *The Peasants' Revolt* (1906)

F. M. Page, *The Estates of Crowland Abbey : A Study in Manorial Organisation* (Cambridge, 1934)

F. Pollock and F. W. Maitland, *The History of English Law Before the Time of Edward I,* Second Edition (Cambridge, 1923)

E. Simcoe, *Thaxted* (Saffron Walden, 1934)

J. Tait, *The Medieval English Borough* (Manchester, 1936)

J. E. Thorold Rogers, *Six Centuries of Work and Wages* (1909)

P. Vinogradoff, *Villeinage in England* (Oxford, 1892)

C. M. Beresford, 'The Poll Tax Returns of 1377, 1379 and 1381' (*The Amateur Historian*, Vol. 3, No. 7, 1959)

E. M. Carus-Wilson, 'Evidences of Industrial Growth on some Fifteenth-Century Manors' (*The Economic History Review,* Second Series, Vol. XII, No. 2, 1959)

R. H. Hilton, 'Peasant Movements in England before 1381' (*The Economic History Review,* Second Series, Vol. II, No. 2, 1949)

M. Postan, 'Some Economic Evidence of Declining Population in the Later Middle Ages' (*The Economic History Review,* Second Series, Vol. II, No. 3, 1950)

Rev. J. E. Symond, 'Thaxted and its Cutlers Guild' (*Transactions* of the Essex Archaeological Society, Vol. IV (New Series, 1889))

INDEX OF PERSONS

* denotes that there is more than one reference on the same page; an occupation or status assigned to a name in the Poll Tax Return, 1381, is shown in brackets; (——) indicates that the name but no occupation is on the return; (?) that there may have been an occupation given, but it cannot be read because of defects in the document.